UN SCRIPT

UNSCRIPT

The Radical Act of Being Yourself

CHRISTIAN O'CONNELL

WILEY

First published 2026 by John Wiley & Sons Australia, Ltd

ISBN: 978-1-394-41936-4

NATIONAL LIBRARY OF AUSTRALIA

A catalogue record for this book is available from the National Library of Australia

Registered Office
John Wiley & Sons Australia, Ltd. Level 4, 600 Bourke Street, Melbourne, VIC 3000, Australia

For details of our global editorial offices, customer services, and more information about Wiley products visit us at www.wiley.com.

Wiley also publishes its books in a variety of electronic formats and by print-on-demand. Some content that appears in standard print versions of this book may not be available in other formats.

Cover Design by Wiley
Cover Image: © Vita/stock.adobe.com
Author Photo: Nicholas Wilson
Figure 5.1: Radio image: © Suhadi/Adobe Stock

Set in 12/16.5pt and Adobe Garamond Pro by Straive, Chennai, India.

Printed and bound by CPI Group (UK) Ltd, Croydon, CR0 4YY

C9781394419364_100726

The manufacturer's authorized representative according to the EU General Product Safety Regulation is Wiley-VCH GmbH, Boschstr. 12, 69469 Weinheim, Germany, e-mail: Product_Safety@wiley.com.

For Sarah. My home. The one who calls me back to myself.

For Ruby and Lois. My girls. I wrote this for you.

For Jackie. Your last gift lit the spark for this book.

For Rob. Who showed me what happens when we unscript.

For everyone who's ever listened. Thank you for being my purpose.

You trusted me with your stories and your hearts.

It's a joy to be your companion.

And for all the versions of me who've walked into radio studios since 1998—and for all the versions still to come.

Contents

Introduction

The gift in your imperfect story

I'm now friends with the paramedic who came and tried in vain to save my mother-in-law's life.

July 2024 was the worst day of my family's life.

We'd just returned from a family holiday, bags dumped by the door, that happy tiredness still clinging to us. My mother-in-law, Jackie, had been house-sitting. We caught up over a cup of tea, and then my wife, Sarah, drove her mum five minutes back to her place.

Then my younger daughter, Lois, called me, her voice tight with panic.

'Nana has collapsed. This is it, Dad. She's dying, Mum says!'

There are these moments when life splits in two: before the call, after the call. You don't forget the sound of the words, the air you breathed in that instant, the unreality of it. I was sitting in the car we'd just gifted to my eldest daughter Ruby for her twentieth birthday. She'd overheard as I took the call. I told her quickly, clumsily.

Ruby and I drove the short distance to Jackie's house. I begged Ruby not to come inside. I saw my younger daughter Lois out on the street waiting for the ambulance, her face white with fear.

Inside was a scene that didn't feel like my life. Sarah was on the floor performing CPR on her own mum. Guiding her through the phone speaker was the steady, rhythmic voice of a stranger—an anonymous angel counting out compressions with a calm authority. Her voice filled the room with something that cut through the chaos: presence. Counting out the numbers for Sarah to do the chest compressions to. She kept Sarah going—I don't know how she had the strength to continue.

I dropped down onto the floor too, held Jackie's hand with one hand and pressed my other palm to her forehead. I started speaking to her, urging her to stay with us, saying the things we all say when words are flimsy rafts against a flood. Long minutes later, the paramedics arrived. They worked on her with all the urgency and skill in the world, but it was too late. Jackie was gone. We'd been home from the holiday barely 90 minutes.

What followed is hard to describe unless you've lived it—the way time blurs and stretches, the chaos, the helplessness. The utter terror. My daughters were outside, Ruby starting to faint, Lois rooted to the spot. Inside, my wife's world was collapsing. And into this storm walked a paramedic named Rob.

You could feel instantly that he'd been doing this a long time. He wasn't just efficient, he was present. Calm, open, listening, his voice was intentional and slower than the frantic racing of ours. This was a man who'd learned what's needed and what really matters in these devastating moments.

At one point, as we waited for the funeral directors, he asked me what we wanted done with Jackie. I froze. I didn't know. What should we do? This was all so sudden and unexpected.

'What could we do?' I asked, helpless. Rob said softly, 'Well, if it were my mum, I'd want her placed in her bed.' And so that's what they did.

Think about that. He came to treat Jackie, but he ended up treating us. His choice gave Sarah something invaluable: a few precious hours lying beside her mum, cuddling her, talking to her, crying with her.

Time she wouldn't otherwise have had. Time that softened the shock, allowed some love and dignity to sit alongside the loss. That was Rob's gift to us, and it will never leave me.

Later, as the first responders packed up to leave, I stood watching in awe. We only see slices of their work when they come crashing into our lives. But this is their everyday: the drama, the pain, the tears. They can't save everyone. The weight of that must live in their bodies. I knew what the weight of this one loss was already doing to mine.

As I thanked Rob, my voice cracked. Gratitude overcame me. Isn't it true that when we speak from the heart, our voices often betray us? That crack—it's the sound of armour splitting. Breaking open to what's just longing to be felt and expressed. And then Rob said something that changed me. Something I think about almost every day, and that inspired me to write this book.

He said, 'I hope you don't think this is odd ...'

I told him, 'Rob, after the past two hours, nothing could be odd.'

He said he knew who I was. He'd listened to me on *The Imperfects* podcast. *The Imperfects* is one of the biggest podcasts in Australia and it does great work for mental health. He'd heard me talk about my panic attacks. And it had helped him. He said it had made him feel less odd, less alone. It had changed his relationship with his own panic attacks entirely.

Now here's the thing: I'd been worried sick about that podcast. Afterwards, I thought I'd overshared. Gone deeper than I meant to. Said too much. There's still shame in me about that time, about losing control, my fear when I talk about it, looking weak. I worried people would think less of me, or worse: that they'd stop listening. Vulnerability hangovers are real.

But there, in the middle of my family's worst day, Rob told me that the very story I regretted sharing had been exactly the story he needed to hear. The crack I thought was too messy, too exposing, had been an outstretched hand in the dark for him. That story was a bridge between us.

The stories we're most afraid to tell are the ones that matter most. Not the polished anecdotes we rehearse. Not the safe stories that keep us looking shiny. The raw ones. The shaky ones. The ones that make us fear, 'Did I just say too much?'

Those are the stories that transform us and the people we share them with. They remind us of the truth about connection: it doesn't live in our perfection, it lives in our imperfection. It lives not in our strength, but in our willingness to let others see our struggles.

The story I was ashamed of became the story that mattered most. It travelled from me, to a podcast studio, into Rob's ears and then came back to me in my family's darkest hour. It helped me get back into my heart and feel less alone.

Rob could have just done his job and left. Professional. Efficient. Even kind. But instead, he dropped his script about being 'the paramedic' and showed up as Rob: a human being who happened to work as a paramedic. He extended grace to us, and then extended it to himself by sharing his truth.

And in that realness, something unfolded. I unfroze and felt more present to be able to meet this moment and help my girls and poor Sarah.

Weeks later, we went back to the ambulance station to thank the team. Rob looked embarrassed. They hadn't saved Jackie, but they'd treated us like humans when we needed it most.

Rob and I swapped numbers. We've hung out a few times since fate threw us together.

That day changed everything for my family. My daughters experienced their first real loss. My wife lost her beloved mum. But we were also given something: a reminder that true connection is possible even in the worst of it. Maybe especially in the worst of it.

This is what happens when we unscript—when we drop the stories and masks, and the carefully curated personas and identities—and instead show up authentically. When we extend that grace to others too. When we remember that behind every role and title, every carefully constructed image, there's just a person trying to figure it out, same as we are. A person who wants to connect to you.

That night, I was given a gift. Jackie's last gift.

Stop trying to improve

Now, before we go any further, let me take the pressure off both of us.

You don't have to do anything.

You don't have to get anything. You don't have to suddenly start telling stories like a stand-up comedian. You don't have to become so vulnerable in meetings that you start crying in boardrooms.

No expectations.

And from my side? I'm not trying to get you to change. I'm not trying to make you 'speak better'. I'm not here to fix you or improve you or turn you into some polished version of yourself.

Maybe this helps. Maybe it doesn't. Maybe you read this whole book and nothing changes. At least you'll have heard some funny stories, laughed a little and enjoyed our time together. I believe you will start to challenge some assumptions about the scripts you have running, and become more excited about connecting more freely, with more of who you really are.

Because here's what I've learned: *the moment we stop trying to make something happen is usually when it actually happens.*

The tyranny of self-improvement

There's a shadow the self-help movement has created. A kind of tyrannical, anti-human way of seeing yourself as someone who needs fixing. Someone who's not quite good enough yet.

You see it everywhere:

'10× YOUR PRODUCTIVITY'

'THE ULTIMATE MORNING ROUTINE'

'7 HABITS OF HIGHLY EFFECTIVE PEOPLE WHO WAKE UP AT 4 AM AND DRINK YAK PISS COFFEE'

It's exhausting, isn't it?

I don't want to be optimised.

And underneath all of it is this message: you're not acceptable as you are. When you're more productive, when you're more optimised, when you're more healed, more awakened, more whatever—*then* you'll be worthy. *Then* you'll be acceptable.

Part of you rebels against that. The wise, knowing part with the quiet voice. Your true inner wisdom.

Welcome to the *un*-movement

So here's what this book is actually about:

Not improvement. *Unfoldment.*

Not fixing yourself. *Finding yourself.*

Not adding more techniques and strategies and things to master. *Clearing away what's covering your authentic voice.*

Welcome to:

- *un*doing (the scripts that aren't yours)
- *un*learning (the rules that never served you)
- *un*derthinking (getting out of your head)
- *un*coaching (because you're not broken and you don't need fixing).

This is *unscript*.

I'm Christian and I'm your *un*coach.

So, I'm not Tony Robbins.

Well, I'm the Tony Robbins of stumbling through life. Sometimes stumbling over gold, sometimes just stumbling. I believe your magic is in the mess.

I'm not writing this from some mountaintop of mastery. I'm writing this from the middle of the mess, where most of us actually live. And what I've learned over 30 years of doing live radio every single morning is this:

The best moments—in radio, in life, in connection—happen when you stop trying to be good enough, or fit in, and just show up as you are.

How this actually works

Think of this book like we're going on a walk together. Just chatting. Me telling you stories, sharing what I've learned, giving you some frameworks that might help you.

Everything in here I've lived with. No theories. No regurgitated wisdom from courses I took last month.

I have almost three decades worth of speaking, storytelling and stumbling for a living. Both sides of this planet. I'm a master of one thing, of my own life. And so are you.

You don't have to read the chapters in order, though they do build. You don't have to do everything perfectly. You don't even have to finish it if it's not serving you.

The only instruction I have is *stop trying to improve while you're reading this.*

Just be curious. Notice what lands. Feel what shifts in your body. Try the experiments if they interest you. Adopt what feels useful; ditch the rest.

At the end of each chapter, you'll find something I call 'Unfolders': questions designed not to be answered immediately, but to unfold over time. They're not tests. They're just gentle invitations to notice what's already there, hiding under your scripts.

Head to www.christianoconnell.com/unscript for a free downloadable PDF of all Unfolders.

The acorn already knows

And now a quick lesson from acorns and oak trees. Nature is our greatest teacher and reminder of our true nature. I love oak trees. My daughters call me 'the tree nerd'. When they were younger and lived at home, any time they were struggling I used to take them to see oak trees. We'd just chat to them while sitting under them. Magic happened. One of my daughters, before she left home, even got a tattoo of an oak leaf and acorn.

Now they are wise to this and recently I messaged one of them, who was having a tough time, asking to meet me under the oak trees. I got this text back:

> Oh no, not the oaks. That's when you know things are fucked—when Dad's taking you to the oak trees.

Oaks are such mighty trees, towering lords of the tree world. Yet, an acorn doesn't *improve* its way into becoming an oak tree. It doesn't read *7 Habits of Highly Effective Trees.* It doesn't have a morning routine or a productivity hack. Or listen to four-hour podcast episodes titled 10× Your Trunk.

It just unfolds what's already there. Given the right conditions—soil, water, sunlight, air—it becomes what it already is.

You're the same way.

Everything you need to be a powerful, authentic communicator? It's already in you. Your authentic, true voice is already there. Your capacity for genuine connection is already there.

It's just covered up. By scripts you learned. By ideas about who you should be. By trying so hard to be good enough to fit in that you forgot how to just be yourself.

You don't need to become someone new. You need to remember who you already are.

One last thing

This book is your permission slip. To be you, to take up space, to have a voice. To be heard. To know your voice and that what's in your heart matters.

Christian x

Gloriously Unoptimised since 1973

Unfolders

Three questions to sit with, not to answer immediately:

1. What would it feel like to stop trying to improve yourself in some area of your life?
2. Where in your life are you performing 'good enough' instead of just being yourself?
3. What's one script you've been living that you know, deep down, isn't really yours?

PART I
Static

1

We're losing each other

We've never been more connected. And we've never felt more alone.

Your phone buzzes with messages from so many people. You're technically 'in touch' with everyone. And yet, when was the last time you felt truly *seen*? When did someone last look you in the eye and really get you?

We're broadcasting all the time, but nobody's tuning in. We're scrolling through each other's highlight reels while sitting at the dinner table, phones glowing on our faces, nodding along to conversations we're not actually having.

The result? We're losing the very skills that make us human. Empathy. Presence. The ability to sit with someone in their pain or joy and just … *be* there.

But here's what gives me hope: the hunger for something real is stronger than ever. People *know* something's missing. They can feel it. I'm witnessing this from the unique perspective my work gives me. People are starved of real contact and connection. The calls, emails and messages I get now all speak to this. My focus group is real people. They all sense what is happening.

That's what this chapter is about. Waking up to what's happening so we can do something about it.

The mirror

During the dark days of Melbourne's lockdown—remember, we held the title of most locked-down city on Earth—our family discovered *Married at First Sight*. Also known as *MAFS*, which could stand for Mating Absolute Ferals.

For the uninitiated, it's the Olympics of red flags. A social experiment run by producers with wine.

We were hooked. Judging away from our couch, shovelling snacks into our pie holes, feeling wonderfully superior as chaos unfolded on our screen.

But one night, after the final shout and the fade to credits, I picked up the remote and switched the TV off. And there we were—reflected in the black glass.

Still. Slumped. Half-alive.

It hit me: the image on the screen was us.

We were watching ourselves—disconnected, numbed, scrolling through other people's mess to avoid our own.

The TV was a mirror. And I didn't like what I saw.

This isn't just a feeling. Harvard has been tracking people's lives since 1938, the longest study on human happiness ever conducted. After almost 90 years, the finding is crystal clear:

The quality of your relationships determines the quality of your life.

Not your job. Not your money. Not your achievements.

Your relationships.

The people who were most satisfied in their relationships at age 50 were the healthiest at age 80. The lonely ones? They died earlier. Got sicker faster. Their brains deteriorated more quickly.

In 2023, the US Surgeon General called it 'the epidemic of loneliness'. The health risks of prolonged loneliness are equivalent to smoking 15 cigarettes a day. The World Health Organization now calls it a global health crisis.

Relationships aren't optional. They're literally a matter of life and death.

The anti-social century

Derek Thompson, a writer I admire, gave a name to the times we are living in, in his 2025 article, 'The Anti-Social Century'.

He did the maths. Since 2000, we've added 99 minutes of alone time at home every single day compared to a generation ago. That's nearly two hours we used to spend *with* people that we now spend *away* from them.

Here in Australia, 70 per cent of restaurant business is now take-out and delivery. The bar that used to be full of people talking is now full of brown bags waiting for owners who'll never sit down, never talk, never stay.

The ring that's collapsing

Social scientist Marc Dunkelman discovered something crucial: we haven't lost *all* our connections. His 'Three Rings' concept highlights that we've strengthened two while letting a third collapse:

- *The Inner Ring*—your immediate family—is stronger than ever. We text our partners constantly. I can see exactly where my daughters are at all times. They *love* that at 19 and 21.
- *The Outer Ring*—your tribes and communities of interest—are also stronger. Whatever you're into, there's a global digital network for it.

- *The Middle Ring* is collapsing. Your neighbours. The faces on the train, in the coffee shop, at the park. The acquaintances. The weak ties. The village.

And this is the most important ring of all.

Your family teaches you love. Your tribe teaches you loyalty. But the village? *The village teaches you tolerance.*

The village is where you meet people who don't think like you. Where you learn that the person who disagrees with you is still a person with dreams, pain and a heart just like yours.

Without the village, politics goes berserk. We lose the muscle of empathy. We become intolerant of everyone who's not family or tribe.

The disconnection entrepreneurs

Now let's talk about who's profiting from this.

Every platform, every algorithm, every ping and scroll and autoplay episode engineered by some of the smartest behavioural scientists in the world to keep us staring at screens instead of each other.

What's more profitable: you sitting in a pub with mates for three hours? Or you sitting alone, doomscrolling while you're served ads and your data is being harvested?

Scrolling has become the new smoking: addictive, normalised and obscenely profitable.

Our disconnection is their dividend.

Dead words vs living voice

After almost 30 years in radio, I can honestly say I don't think there is any comparison between text and voice. None.

Text is static. Voice is alive.

I don't mean that as a metaphor. I mean it literally, scientifically.

When you text someone, you're sending symbols. Static marks on a screen. And here's what the research tells us: *words themselves only account for about 7 per cent of the meaning in human communication.*

Seven per cent.

So what's the other 93 per cent? Some of it is body language. More of it is one of my obsessions (which we will get to): the energetics of speaking. But first, let me tell you about *paralinguistics*. Basically, everything your voice does *beyond* the words. Your tone. Your pitch. Your pace. Your pauses. Your volume. Your inflection. The little catch in your breath. The warmth or coldness in your delivery. The frequency on which your words are carried matters more than your words.

When you hear someone's voice, you're not just processing their words. You're reading their emotional state, their confidence or uncertainty, their connection to what they're saying. You're picking up hundreds of micro-signals that answer the questions, Can I trust this person? Are they joking or serious? Are they open or closed? Are they present with me or performing for me?

Your voice carries your humanity. It's your soul manifest.

Think about it. The text that read as angry when it was meant to be funny? That's because you lost the 93 per cent. The emoji that can't quite capture what you're feeling? That's because thumbs-up and heart symbols can't replicate the warmth in your voice when you say, 'I'm proud of you'. (Nor can anything capture the chill when my wife calls to say 'You forgot the bins'.)

But there's more to it than that. Neuroscience research shows that when we hear a human voice—a real, authentic human voice—our brains light up in ways they don't with text or synthesised speech.

Results of studies using MRI scans published in the journal *Proceedings of the Royal Society B* revealed that hearing someone's voice activates regions of the brain associated with empathy, emotional processing and social connection. Your brain is literally wired to respond to the human voice in a way it doesn't respond to written words. When you hear someone laugh, your brain releases oxytocin, the bonding hormone. When you hear warmth in someone's voice, your nervous system begins to co-regulate with theirs. You literally sync up. Heart rates synchronise. Breathing patterns align.

This is what human connection looks like at a physiological level. We are hardwired to connect.

And we're trading it for 'lol' and thumbs-up emojis.

The train experiment

Here's where it gets interesting.

Researcher Nicholas Epley offered commuters on trains in Chicago three options to try: talk to someone nearby, do whatever you normally do or enjoy your solitude.

He asked them to predict which option would make them happiest. Almost everyone predicted solitude.

They were all wrong.

The people who talked to strangers reported being significantly happier. Every single time.

But Epley thought maybe Chicago people are just friendly. So he went to test his result in the grumpiest place he could think of.

London.

My old town! London commuters are *notoriously* crabby. The tube has an unwritten rule: eye contact is basically assault.

And you know what he found?

Same result.

Even grumpy Londoners were happier after talking to a stranger.

Here's the part that explains everything. When Epley dug deeper, he found that people didn't think *the other person* would enjoy the conversation. They thought *the other person didn't want to talk to them.*

Everyone on the train thinks they're the only one who wants to talk. Everyone assumes everyone else wants to be left alone.

Epley calls it 'pluralistic ignorance': we're all following the same invisible script, all waiting for someone else to go first.

That moment when you look at someone, feel that impulse to say something, then look away at your phone—that's not you making a choice. That's the script choosing for you.

And the script is lying. The other person wants to talk too.

My Uber lab

I experienced this firsthand.

Last year was intense at work. I started taking Ubers in the morning rather than driving. One morning—tired, pressure on, feeling alone—I risked a small conversation instead of sealing myself off with AirPods.

It lit my driver up. It lit me up.

When we pulled up, the young guy turned and thanked me for the chat. A quick handshake. That look. The kind a bot or text can't touch. We felt our shared humanity. My tension dissolved. I skipped into the studio.

Now that ride is a ritual, a human warm-up. My social WD-40.

I met a driver with the surname 'Ufuk'. I asked about it and he told me how problematic life with that surname is. Girlfriends laugh. So he changed his name.

'Well done,' I said. 'What is it now?'

'Yeah, I changed it to Matthew Ufuk.'

Wait. You changed your *first* name? You thought *that* was the problem?

Yes, he did. Love this man.

Another driver, very articulate, asked if I worry about what to say on radio. 'No,' I told him. 'If you pay attention to your life, there's always something to say.'

He said his life is boring. Impossible. I asked about his other job: selling home insurance. 'Any weird claims?'

Jackpot. A woman in a second-floor shower fell through the floor into the kitchen below. Then an elderly lady on the toilet—same thing—straight through.

Our lives are far from boring. Being human is endlessly fascinating.

The rebel act

We're living in a culture of curation. Every post, every photo is carefully edited for likes. And that energy doesn't stay online. You start 'performing' yourself everywhere.

Meanwhile, people are starving for real connection. Not content. *Connection.* Not information. *Transformation.*

The algorithms aren't designed to help you see wisely. They're designed to produce anger, fear, division—whatever keeps you scrolling.

You can outsource what you do. You can outsource how you think.

But you cannot outsource who you are.

Fuck the algorithm. Speak to strangers on trains. Ask the question everyone's thinking but nobody's saying. Show up without a script. Be present with your kids—not perfect, just present. Let people see you. Say 'I don't know' when you don't know. Stop rehearsing and start responding.

In a world that profits from your performance, your disconnection, your constant fear that you're not enough, *being real is revolutionary.*

The most radical act you can perform right now is showing up as yourself.

The disconnection entrepreneurs—every platform, every algorithm, every system built to keep you scrolling, performing, outsourcing who you are—they're counting on you staying asleep. Following the script. Choosing comfort over connection. Every single time.

I'm betting you're ready to wake up.

Unfolders

Three questions to sit with, not to answer immediately:

1. What script are you following that you never consciously chose? When you're on the train, in the elevator, at the coffee shop, what invisible rule tells you to look away instead of looking up?
2. Look at your last week. How much time did you spend with other humans, in person, using your living voice? What does this reveal about your actual values?
3. Think of a great conversation you've had recently. What made it so good?

2

He had a dream, not a script

It's 1986, a Saturday night in my family's little living room. Mum and Dad are watching TV. I'm watching them watching TV.

There's a big hairy Scottish man on screen with the wild-eyed energy of a shaman, telling stories and making observations about life that are so honest and so funny, they're making Mum and Dad laugh louder and harder than I've ever seen before. The kind of laughter that shakes the room and makes you feel that, just for a while, everything is right with the world.

That man was Billy Connolly.

I'd never seen anyone like him.

He wasn't like other TV comics. His stories meandered, roaming anywhere and everywhere. Midstream, he'd lose his way—or pivot completely. He swore. He didn't just tell stories; he lived them as he told them.

Most of all, what impressed young me is that he was making it all up. Off the top of his head.

I kept annoying Dad, asking, 'How is he doing this? How is he just... making it all up?'

While talking—with so much contagious energy and emotion—he would suddenly make himself laugh as he discovered words tumbling out of his mouth, surprised at what he was overhearing himself say.

That was the magic. He was as delighted by what was coming through him as were we.

He wasn't performing comedy. He was channelling it.

And something in my 13-year-old brain lit up: *Oh. You can do that. You can just… let it come through you.*

I didn't know it at 13, watching Billy Connolly, but I was witnessing what would become my life's work: talking into a microphone, telling stories and sharing observations about life and what it is to be us.

I've spent my life chasing that feeling. That aliveness. That magic of words finding you instead of you finding words.

Maybe that's why I've always been obsessed with great speeches: moments when words become electric.

I've even got an entire YouTube playlist of great speeches from TV shows, movies and real life. There's President Jed Bartlet raging at God in a cathedral on *The West Wing*; Al Pacino's half-time sermon in *Any Given Sunday*—which still gets me every time—and, of course, the real ones: the moments that shook history.

Like Dr Martin Luther King Jr on the steps of the Lincoln Memorial.

I read a book about that speech once, just to understand what really happened that day. What I found changed how I think about speaking, about presence, about finding your voice.

Because what happened that day wasn't performance. It was transmission.

It was unscripted.

A moment in history

Most people don't realise that only the first half of Martin Luther King Jr's 'I Have a Dream' speech was written, edited and rehearsed. The night before, he'd been in a hotel room surrounded by well-meaning advisors, each with their own agenda: their own lines they hoped would make it into history. A speechwriter, Clarence B Jones, sat there trying to make sense of the competing voices and distil them into a single draft that King could deliver on the steps of the Lincoln Memorial.

By morning, the script was done. The press had copies. The words were fixed.

And yet, the words that changed the world weren't in that script.

The moment everything shifted

When you watch the speech now, look closely. In the opening minutes, King's eyes drop down often: he's reading, staying faithful to the prepared text.

Then something happens. He pauses.

From behind him, the great gospel singer Mahalia Jackson shouts, 'Tell 'em about the dream!'

Not many heard her. King did.

And at that moment he pushes the script aside.

He looks up.

He opens himself to something larger moving through him.

His voice rises. His whole body changes shape—no longer a man giving a speech, but a vessel letting spirit speak through him.

He begins to riff, like a jazz musician catching a melody or a surfer riding down the face of a big wave.

'I have a dream … '

Over and over, he rides the rhythm of it, each repetition building power, momentum, soul. This wasn't memorised. It was remembered—pulled from somewhere deep inside him. A truth he had lived, not learned.

Clarence Jones, standing nearby, whispered to the person next to him, 'These people don't know it yet, but they're about to go to church'.

And they did.

The difference between reading and rising

We've all seen it: leaders, executives, even performers glued to their notes, clinging to their slides, terrified of stepping beyond the safety of the script. Everything is correct. Everything is polished. Everything is safe.

And yet, nothing moves. We aren't moved by what they are saying. They try to lead with logic, and that means they will be met with logic. It becomes brains talking to brains. More data in a day that's already drowning in the stuff.

When I work with people on speaking, I can almost feel the moment when their soul stops talking and their head takes over. The words keep coming, but the energy leaves the room. Because aliveness doesn't live in rehearsed lines — it lives in risk. In uncertainty.

When you stop trying to impress and start allowing what's wanting to be expressed, something holy happens. Your words stop being information and start becoming transmission.

That's what it means to be alive on stage, in a meeting, on air, or in life.

King had been working on another speech for months before this. Mahalia Jackson's heckle — the world's greatest heckle — was reminding him of that one. He didn't need to go find it; he didn't need to reconnect to it. He needed to share it. And his words: they're a full-bodied thing, aren't they? His words, energy, emotion — this is speaking authentically.

Pete sent me

In the first year of my show in Australia, I received an email from a listener, Peter Logan. He had terminal bowel cancer.

Pete asked if I'd read his letter on air, to warn people to do what Australians call 'the poo test': the free bowel screening kit the government starts sending you when you turn 50. The one hardly anyone bothers with.

He hadn't done it. And it would sadly cost him his life. He had so much shame and regret—and he was motivated to make his mistake mean something, to save others. He just needed a platform.

His email was so honest, so moving. I also felt honoured that he'd trusted me with his story. I called him that night and invited him to come on the show. He should share his own story rather than have me read his email out. Hearing his voice would move people more—and give Pete the gift of being in service.

My team weren't so sure. 'You don't have the ratings yet to take a risk like this,' they said. One of them added, 'No-one wants to hear about cancer—bowel cancer—at 8 in the morning'.

Fair point. But no-one ever wants to hear about cancer. It lives in the shadows.

I started to doubt myself. Then I remembered: I'm committed to being more authentic on this show than I've ever been before. And there is no deepening of connection without vulnerability.

Pete came in. He had notes. Pages of them.

I asked if I could see them. I looked at him and said, 'Here's the best thing you can do with these'.

And I tore them up.

'You just need to speak from here,' I said, putting my hand on his racing chest. 'Like you did on the phone.'

He did. He was funny and open. He shared his story. He asked people to do the test and not be like him. He made me cry live on air. At the end of the show, I asked him what he had come here to say. Talk about speaking from the heart! He pointed to his two beautiful daughters, both in their 20s, and said he wouldn't live to walk them down the aisle.

Let's take a breath after that.

A few weeks later, I got a call from someone at the Cancer Council, excitedly saying something miraculous had happened. She went on to say that thanks to Pete's vulnerable story, there was a 600 per cent increase in returned bowel screening kits across the state.

I asked how she knew this, and she reminded me that live on air Pete had said, 'Do the test. Don't end up like me. Send it off and write on the back, "Pete sent me" so I'll know some good came from this'.

Pete sent me. Six hundred per cent.

When we speak from the heart, authentically, it moves people.

A few days before he died, I went to see Pete. We shared a beer. He joked that some good news is that he'd be dead before he had to watch Arsenal's rivals lift the cup, which made me spit out my beer.

That night was the last time I heard from him. He emailed me one last time, thanking me for giving meaning to his mistake. His final line sits on a note on my desk:

Keep up the humour, don't forget the human.

That line broke my heart wide open. It still does.

Some stories stay for life. Pete's is one of mine.

We talk a lot about 'finding your voice'. But the truth is, your voice isn't something you find—it's something you remember. Something you allow. It's the sound of you when you stop trying to be someone else.

Billy Connolly in my parents' living room. King on those steps. Pete in my studio with his notes torn up and his hand on his heart.

Same thing. Same magic.

They weren't performing. They were transmitting.

You don't need a crowd of 250 000 to have your own moment like this. It can happen in a meeting. In a conversation. In a quiet moment with your child. On a morning when you're scared and tired but show up anyway.

Next time you feel that tug—that whisper of something unsaid, that flicker of emotion you want to hide—pause. Push the notes aside. Take a breath. Look up.

Tell them about your dream.

It doesn't have to sound perfect. It just has to sound like you.

He had a dream, not a script.

And remember: keep up the humour, don't forget the human.

Pete sent me.

Unfolders

For these to work best, do this with a kind and generous heart. Watch the judgements—enjoy pulling the threads.

1. *Where in your life are you still reading from a script that no longer fits?* When you're in that meeting, giving that presentation, having that conversation. What invisible script tells you to play it safe instead of speaking truth?
2. *What's your 'Mahalia Jackson' moment?* Who or what has whispered to you, 'Tell them about the dream'—and did you listen? What would it cost you to listen next time?
3. *When have you felt most alive, most present, most unscripted?* What was happening? What did it feel like in your body? What if that way of being wasn't the exception, but the practice?

3

No-one invited you

Spoiler alert! This all turns out okay in the end...

My first radio show in Melbourne. Ten minutes in.

A text comes through: 'Fuck off home'.

Three words. Devastating word economy.

That's not the one that stung though. That one came during my second show, when it got better. (That is, if by better, you mean after the show you message your old therapist in the UK saying you need some help asap.)

I get an email. One of my first ones. How exciting! Think about what that takes. Someone had to find my email address, type it out, check for typos and hit send—all before 7 am, before the call of work kicks in. Plenty of time for emotions to shift, for perspective to arrive, for the adult part of the brain to say, 'Maybe I won't send this'.

But no.

Top of their to-do list that morning was to email me and say:

'No-one invited you'.

Uffff.

I'm sorry, but that's like a heat-seeking missile aimed straight for your heart. No matter what inner work you may have done, that email hits hard. Even Eckhart Tolle himself would've crumbled getting that at 6.22 am. I also love the fact that 22 minutes into my show, two songs and two breaks down, this guy just snaps. *That's it!*

No-one invited you.

Right in the hurt locker.

Suddenly I was 10 again. At school. Trying to fit in. Like we all were. You learn to try and contort yourself into an acceptable shape or persona to fit in, to be accepted.

No-one invited you?

You don't fit in. You don't belong here.

Don't forget, I was on air when this arrived. I had to smile and pretend this was going well. That people liked me.

Adult life is like school sometimes, isn't it?

Two weeks earlier, I'd said goodbye to my audience of 2.5 million in the UK. People whose lives I'd been in for years. Through births, deaths, weddings, divorces. I'd been a constant.

In 14 days I'd gone from national treasure to national trespasser.

Also, in the first two days of my Australian radio career I received some more fan mail. The killer line in this one was, *'You're just a clown without a circus'*.

One thing I was learning was that Australia's trolling is next level. Also, what's sadder than a clown without their circus? It sounds like a Taylor Swift song, 'Clown Without a Circus.'

When my old therapist in the UK woke up and his first message was from his old client now down under as frontier DJ, he set up a Zoom session right away. When I read him the messages, he burst out laughing. I'm talking about slapping-his-thigh laughing.

'Wait, wait, read that clown one again,' he said, wiping his eyes.

I did. He laughed harder. I started to get mad, read it again and he laughed hard again. It was just what I needed. To pay someone to laugh at me.

Let me tell you about Australian radio: it's mad.

It's like *Squid Game.* Every quarter someone doesn't make it. You can be number one on Friday and unemployed by Monday. Radio in the UK is competitive, but not like here. Ratings in the UK come every three months. Here? Try every five weeks. I arrived in July, a few months before what they cheerfully call 'The Killing Season'—October and November—when stations kill off shows that aren't working.

In the UK, at 6 am we talked about the weather: grey with a chance of more grey. In Australia, it's two-for-one specials at Sexyland before sunrise. Back home, radio ads sold garden furniture. Here it is marital aids and erectile dysfunction pills while people are eating Vegemite on toast.

Some kind of calling

I get asked all the time why I left a successful number one rating show to start again as an unknown. The way it's asked, it's as if they think I fled to Australia to escape some scandal.

The truth was, my wife Sarah and I reached our mid-40s and saw the arc of our lives: our daughters would become teenagers, leave home for university and then... wait... is the exciting part of our lives over? Our lives together had been an adventure. Sarah met me, we married and I got offered my first radio job. She quit her job as a lawyer and we moved around the UK three times over the following three years. We loved it.

But that felt a long way in the past. I was in my 40s and one thing I'll say about that decade of your life: shit gets real.

I felt at work I'd started performing a very successful impersonation of myself. I was doing the show; it was easy. But I wasn't really fully there.

I'd spent two decades building a persona that worked. Funny, fast, polished, familiar, smart-arse. I knew what landed, what got laughs, what created connection. I had the timing down to the second. The ratings were number one and I'd won every award going, several times.

But somewhere along the way, I'd lost contact with my creative fire—that spark that used to make me feel alive on air. I felt something had calcified, I felt stuck in my act. A successful one I'd been rewarded for.

I wasn't present anymore.

I was performing an identity.

You know this feeling, right? When you've gotten so good at being who people expect you to be, that you've lost contact with who you actually are. When your life looks successful from the outside but feels a little hollow from the inside.

I tried to distract myself from this growing restlessness. Suddenly, drinking wine on a Monday night and eating a kilo of cheese was a good idea. I launched stand-up tours. Wrote kids' books. Loved all of these, genuinely. They were good distractions.

But there it was. The calling. Although at the time I misread it as a feeling of unease. It scared me.

A calling is hard to explain. It's not a voice. It's not a plan. It's a deep knowing of what to do next, even when what's next makes no logical sense.

These callings—when you're brave enough to answer them—actually guide you closer to who you are.

To not answer this calling would have been to deny life itself.

But that's where the calling was leading me. It was the same for my wife Sarah.

And I'd learned something over the years: when you feel that pull, that deep resonance in your body that says 'this way', you have to follow it. Even when everyone thinks you're mad.

Because your life can become an adventure again, instead of a performance to manage.

And now, here on the other side of the world, that identity was gone. The successful national radio host—Mr Number 1—destroyed.

The accent, the safety, the certainty—stripped away.

Every morning I'd sit in that studio with nothing. No shared history to reference. No familiar voices calling in. No accumulated goodwill to draw on. Just me and a microphone and a city that, it felt like, didn't want me there.

It was a crucible moment: from 2.5 million listeners who knew my voice intimately, to strangers who only heard difference.

That's the kind of fire that burns away everything except what's essential about connection. We've all experienced what it feels like when your life is on fire, raging out of control. I've had burnout throughout my life.

But sometimes, when it's done right with support, you can find growth in the fire.

Your crucible, a crossroads you're at in your life: it might be divorce, unemployment, illness, becoming a parent, losing a parent. Any moment when the snow globe of your life gets violently shaken up, or smashed completely. What you thought you knew stops working and you're forced to find out what's actually true underneath. It can be a transformative experience. It will require a huge amount of vulnerability, and if being vulnerable was easy, the world wouldn't look like it does right now.

Finding my new voice

We all talk about imposter syndrome. I was living it. An actual imposter. That email—'No-one invited you'—felt like the whole country was saying it.

A few days before I started on air, I'm joining a new doctor's surgery. There's a receptionist there, telling me how multicultural Melbourne is, how welcoming, how diverse.

Then she asks what I'll be doing in Australia.

'Breakfast radio,' I say.

She looks at me, genuinely confused. 'How will that work?' she asks. 'You've got a foreign voice.'

Not accent. Voice.

My voice—the instrument I'd spent 20 years crafting, the thing that had connected me to millions of people—was wrong here. Foreign. Other. It was my living.

I went home that night and thanked that old crone on reception. She helped me get clarity on what I needed to do. Because life is always speaking to us. Even if it's not what we want to hear.

Right then, when I thought about how I could win them over, make a connection, I imagined a Venn diagram: one circle was me, the other circle was the listeners I wanted to connect to.

The overlap—that sweet spot—was what I had to find.

What's universal? What's undeniable?

This overlap between us—sector, is that bit called? Vector? Quadrant? I failed maths at school. Let's say sector. It's my book, so my rules.

Anyway, the Venn overlap, that would be my gateway drugs. Once I met them there, I could connect and I'd have them. So I became a dealer, and I was dealing vibes.

This wasn't so much about starting a new show. It was about making people feel something. Establishing an emotional connection.

That was the frequency I'd lost. Not technique. Not skill. The emotional wavelength underneath all the words. To start to do what I love doing: telling stories. And life right now was nothing but stories.

So I began small.

Stories about being a dad to daughters.

A husband.

An outsider trying to find his place.

The elephant in the room was me being a Brit on Australian radio. I owned it. Talked about it. Made jokes about it. I saw Australians with fresh eyes: the customs and rituals of life here. How they behave, things they wouldn't even be aware of. They loved hearing my observations and questions. Because I was being in wonder. Most of our day we are running on scripts and automatic programs. We kind of sleepwalk through much of our day. My job is to pay attention. Be in wonder.

I started to be more open, raw and honest than ever before. I started speaking from my heart. Now by that I don't mean everything being deadly serious — I mean speaking more authentically.

The frequency of authenticity is greater than love

There's a principle in physics called constructive interference. When two waves of similar frequency meet, they don't cancel each other — they amplify. The energy doubles.

That's what great conversation feels like. Two honest signals meet, and something larger than either person emerges. You both leave more alive. This means you can draw energy from people, and they from you. When two people are both tuned to authenticity, both broadcasting from presence rather than performance, their frequencies don't compete — they amplify.

But here's where it gets even more interesting.

Research on human emotional states has found something interesting. Love and joy rank high, but authenticity ranks even higher.

Authenticity is the single most powerful frequency a human being can emit. Forty times stronger than love and joy.

People are astonishingly good at detecting congruence — that is, whether what you say matches what you feel. Emotional states spread (that's called emotional contagion) and attention deepens around presence. Whether you call it 'vibes' or 'nervous system cues', everyone in the room is reading your signal.

When you unscript, you don't find yourself—you expand into more of yourself. A fuller expression of you. When something happened with my kids, I talked about it not as a 'bit' (that's what we call a little routine in broadcasting: before the show, we meet and swap what bits we may have for that day's show) but as a real thing I was navigating. Talking it over out loud. Trying to explore my world and life with my words. When I didn't understand something about Australian culture, I didn't pretend. I asked. When I felt like an outsider, I said it.

I spoke about how hard I was finding it making new friends. My wife wasn't struggling, but I was.

I even asked a friendly Uber driver out for a beer. He never replied to my text. Another low point. If I couldn't get a taxi driver to like me, what hope for a city?

Slowly, the tone shifted. I didn't need my gateway drugs so much.

A new kind of connection began to emerge: I was showing up less guarded, less curated and way more authentically than I had been before. I was loving it. I felt freer than I had in a long time. The joy of unscripting. I felt more playful.

What was interesting was the effect it was having on my audience. They were sharing funny stories. Trusting me because they felt safe with me and the atmosphere I was creating. Being more vulnerable helped me open up deeper ways to be funny, and connect better. The more I talked about real life, the more calls and interaction I got. I was getting more calls than I ever got in the UK.

This was contagious authenticity.

Something extraordinary happened: people started responding not to the professional broadcaster, not to the Pom, but to the human being who was stumbling along just like them. I saw firsthand that being authentic is magnetic.

During my third week on air, word reached me from a former colleague. They'd been in a boardroom meeting at a rival station. Someone had played clips from my show. After listening, one of the executives had solemnly declared, 'Unlikely he'll make it to the end of the year'.

My colleague apologised when they told me, like a doctor presenting you with a terminal diagnosis.

I thanked them.

It fuelled me. Anger, when channelled right, is a powerful force. They'd said it was 'unlikely' I'd see the new year on air so I renamed our team's WhatsApp group: 'The Unlikelies'.

I doubled-down on being undeniable.

And of course, uninvited.

Many mornings in the first few months on the way in to work, I'd feel almost physically weighed down with the pressure of carrying the show. The endless pressure of ratings to survive.

One morning, at traffic lights, I could feel a dread rising up in me physically. The girls were struggling to fit in at their new schools. Sarah was holding everything together and I was carrying this script in my head: *You have to be great at 6 am. You have to carry the show alone. You can't tell them this is hard. Be strong. Be funny. This has to work or you'll be fired. No-one invited you.*

There are two voices in our life: the one we say out loud and the one in our head.

Then I looked at the other people stopped at the lights. I wondered who they were, the paths they'd walked to get here. What they'd struggled with, loved, lost, dreamed about.

I felt this warm glow of connection. Of something shared between us.

I'd been turning them — the listeners — into this demanding entity, always hungry, always judging. But then I saw myself in these beautiful people at the lights and wondered, Would they want me to feel this stress and pressure? No.

When I dropped the script of 'I'm alone, I have to do it all myself', everything shifted.

Then a powerful image came to me: sitting around a campfire in the morning. A large circle. I was in the circle, but I wasn't above it on a throne. Some radio shows are like a pyramid and someone like me is at the top of the pyramid talking down to people lucky to hear their words. I was in a circle, part of it. Not above it.

My job, I saw then, was just to start the fire, and let the fire be a warm welcome to those needing warmth and safety around my fire. The very things I needed. I shifted from 'it's all on me' to co-creation and collaboration.

Then what happens around fires? Great conversations. Stories. Laughter. Sharing.

I don't have to carry the show. I just light the fire.

Wait, can I turn the lens around?

For most of the first 12 months, my nervous system was stuck on red alert, I had panic attacks before most shows and a constant voice was asking, 'Am I good enough to make this work?'

Then I had a session with a woman who did healing work on your energy body. Look, I know, I know. I'm a closeted woo-woo guy. But I'll try anything, and she was incredible.

At the end of the session, she said, 'This phrase came through for you: "When I get nervous, I focus on service"'.

My whole body exhaled. Like every cell had been holding its breath since I landed in this country, and suddenly it could let go.

It was so simple, but it changed everything. Because I'd had the lens pointing the wrong way: at me.

'Am I good enough? Am I doing this right? Am I going to fail?' All inward. All self-focused. All about protecting myself from humiliation.

But I could turn that lens around.

When your heart is open and you focus on contribution—on co-creation, on genuinely serving the people listening—doubt dissolves. Because you're not thinking about you anymore. You're thinking about *them*.

That shift—from performance to service, from self-protection to open-heartedness—it didn't just help with the imposter feelings. It lessened the panic attacks.

Because here's the truth: you can't serve people authentically while simultaneously trying to prove you're good enough to serve them. Those two intentions can't coexist.

One is about you. The other is about them.

One contracts. The other expands.

And the most beautiful part? When I stopped trying to prove I belonged and started focusing on what I could give, people responded. Not because I'd suddenly become more competent or more Australian or more 'right' for the job.

Because I'd become more present. More real. More *there* with them.

That's the frequency people tune into. Not competence. *Presence.* Not performance. *Connection.* Not proving. *Serving.*

The biggest exile wasn't being 10 000 miles away from home.

It was being exiled from myself.

I'd developed chameleon skills—always adapting, fitting in, reading the room. We do this, don't we? Betray ourselves. I'd betrayed myself in little ways on TV shows, in meetings, on air.

I not only felt like I didn't belong, I was being *told* I didn't belong. And what I felt underneath that was that I'd been feeling a lack of belonging for a while, even back home.

The lesson came slowly, but clearly.

Belonging doesn't come from fitting in. It comes from belonging to yourself first. It comes from coming home to yourself.

The calling had been right all along. It was leading me home. Just not to the home I thought.

Somewhere along that road—between 'fuck off home' and hitting number one, between the panic attacks and the campfires—I stopped *trying* to connect.

Connection became something I *was*.

Unfolders

Sit with these questions. Don't rush to answer them. Let them unfold in you.

1. Where in your life are you still waiting for an invitation? What are you not doing, not saying, not being because you're waiting for permission? From whom? And what would change if you invited yourself?
2. What calling have you been distracting yourself from?
3. What are you in service of? What are you called to serve?

4

The magic of connection

I used to think the really good shows were about preparation and performance. They weren't. They were about presence. Which means they were the result of connection.

Connection: The master frequency

It took me decades to understand this. Some days I'd prepare obsessively, perform my heart out—and the show wouldn't ignite. Then other days I'd walk in exhausted, underprepared, just *there* with whatever was happening—and magic would happen.

There was something real flowing between me and my team, guests, callers and the audience. The lightning jokes, references, call backs, stories and ad libs, all arising from being in connection.

And here's the great news: it's a state you can enter or drop into anytime. A frequency that's always available to you.

A few seconds of weightlessness

Jerry Seinfeld said something in an interview with me that I think about often.

I asked him, 'What's it like, making someone laugh?'

He paused. Then said, 'A few seconds of weightlessness'.

Years later, that line still moves me deeply. Honestly, that's what I could have called this book.

A few seconds of weightlessness.

A few seconds where life lifts you out of your separateness.

A few seconds where two people rise together.

That's what connection feels like. Not performing. Not impressing. Just two people, present together, creating something neither could create alone.

That's what we're chasing.

There's a thought experiment that will bend your mind. I learned it from Joe Hudson, one of the world's most in-demand coaches to leaders and CEOs.

He asked me, 'How much would you have to be paid to give up half your ability to connect with people?'

Really sit with that…

Someone offers you money—any amount you can imagine—but in exchange, your capacity for connection gets cut by 50 per cent. You can still connect, but only at half the depth, half the warmth, half the presence you have now.

How much is that worth?

When I first heard that question, my brain froze. Because once you really think about it, the answer is obvious. There's no amount of money that makes that trade worth it.

There's no amount of millions or billions I would trade for losing my ability to connect with myself, other people, my wife, daughters, sister, mum and dad. Friends, teammates, strangers. With my joy, with my sadness. You'd have nothing in life if you didn't have your ability to connect.

That's when you realise: connection is the most priceless thing you have.

And this isn't just philosophy. There's science behind it.

The longest study ever done

Remember the Harvard study from chapter 1? Eighty-five years of tracking what makes people happy, healthy and fulfilled. The finding: good relationships get into our bodies and keep us alive.

Here's what I also found really moving. When the researchers asked them what they wished they'd done differently, the men said they wished they hadn't spent so much time at work. The women said they wished they hadn't worried so much about what people thought of them.

And when they asked what these people were most proud of? Every single answer was about relationships. Being a good parent. A good partner. A good friend. Not the promotions. Not the awards. Not the money in the bank.

The connections.

And here's the kicker: most of us are giving it away for free. We're trading the connection available in this moment for some imaginary future connection. 'After I get the promotion, *then* I'll have time for my family. After I prove myself, *then* I can relax and connect.'

But that future never comes. Because if your connection is conditional—if it depends on something happening first—you can never actually have it.

You're holding your own heart hostage.

People think being in connection is when everything's plugged in and going really well. Almost like it's another word for flow.

That isn't true.

Connection is the engine that's driving everything.

You can be in connection and be pissed off.

Sometimes—you might be surprised to know—when that alarm goes off at 12 minutes past four in the morning, I don't leap out of bed cartwheeling through the house. I'm tired, overwhelmed, cranky. There are no comedy clubs open at 6 am for a reason.

Everything gets harder for me if I deny that or if I don't allow myself to feel it. But if I let it in—if I get really connected to that crankiness: 'Fuck, I'm tired, I don't feel like being funny for three hours'— if I get in touch with that, if I allow it... it shifts. It moves through me.

And what's on the other side of that? Energy. More energy.

Connection isn't about feeling good all the time. It's about being connected to whatever you're actually feeling. To what's here, present right now.

You can be in connection and be heartbroken and sad. You can be in connection when you're weeping, sobbing, crying. When you're angry. When you're terrified. When you're wildly joyful.

Connection is a meta state. It encompasses all other states.

Being in connection with yourself is the first thing. You can't be connected to other people before being connected to yourself.

The people you're talking to will be able to find you if you can find yourself first.

Team first

For me, the game changer in how I lead my team happened last year.

For a very long time, my number one team principle has always been the show. The quality of the show. The ideas. The performance. Show first.

I was off over Christmas, and thinking about the year just gone. I realised the team hadn't been working comfortably over the year.

Something wasn't right. It wasn't working efficiently. And I asked myself, 'What's my part in this?'

It's very easy to look at other people. But I needed to connect to myself first. What thoughts, what preconceptions did I have that weren't helping? What script did I have in my head about the team, the show, how I led?

Then I wrote down my new guiding principles for the show for the coming year.

I found myself writing at number one 'Team first'.

At first, I scribbled it out.

I can't say that to them, I thought. I'm ashamed to say I thought if I told them that, they'd almost put their feet up on the desk and take it easy. They wouldn't work as hard.

Then I wrote it down again and examined that thought. That script. Is that true? Do any of my team really come to work not to do good work? Why would they want to do that? Don't they want to feel the impact of their work and contribution?

So I shifted to a sense of empowering them more, individually and collectively. 'I need a team of self-leaders. They're on my team because I know they want to do good work. They really care. They care as much as I do.'

Team first.

I always have an offsite team meeting in January before we start the show. I hire a room at the Melbourne Cricket Ground (MCG), an amazing colosseum of sport and music. When it's empty, there's something really unique about it. Almost like a cathedral.

That year, I did it differently.

I said to the team, 'So much of running a team, running a business, is decision making and relationships. And if I could make explicit what's in my head, that would help you make decisions when I'm not around.

Otherwise, you're constantly trying to second-guess what I would do. And that must be exhausting and confusing.

'So I've written down these guiding principles for the team. And this is the most important one. This is it.'

I paused.

'Team first.'

I was about to move on, but first I looked around the group. They were stunned.

Maybe they had misheard me. So I said it again. 'I said number one: it's team first.'

And I could feel the energy in the circle just open up. Like heart space expanding.

One of them put their notepad down. Eyes glistened. 'Wow. Really wasn't expecting that from you.'

Then someone else. 'Yeah.' They also put their notepad down. The group made a collective sigh of relief. I could feel their nervous systems high fiving each other.

It was a really vulnerable, open moment. I had no idea we'd get there.

I felt it. And I said, 'I'm really sorry, guys. I didn't realise that maybe I've been adding tension, running this team in a kind of dysfunctional way by always driving performance. I thought that's how you had to be. That's how I was with myself, I guess.

'But actually, the health of this team — us being connected — that's the number one priority now. Because if you look at our best shows, it's always upstream when the team is working well. It's never the other way around.

'Great shows are never because I'm yelling, "Work harder, be funnier, have better ideas". It's actually because we're enjoying it more.'

Then we had a really big, open chat. And I said, 'I think I really need to open myself up more. Be more connected to the truth. I always think you guys can't handle it when I'm stressed or overwhelmed.'

And they said, 'We'd like to help more. Sometimes we can see you're carrying something alone. You don't need to do that'.

Yeah. Connection.

What code are you speaking, Chris?

Connection is a full-body sport. You have to be deeply connected to your inner landscape, to what's going on in your body. Your body is speaking to you. If you're connected, you can hear when there's tension somewhere—your body is signalling: offering information, guidance.

I'm still learning this. Let me tell you about one Sunday.

My daughters had come home for a lovely dinner. So nice. Then they left to go back to university.

And I had this tremendous emptiness.

I thought the best thing—rather than share this with my wife—was to go to the cinema and watch a big, noisy movie. I went to see *F1*, the Brad Pitt film.

Anyway, I'm watching Brad Pitt's character facing his past, connecting with it, and I start to get emotional. I look around—no-one else is teary eyed. And I'm thinking, I don't think this is about Brad Pitt.

I'm crying because I'm missing my daughters. They're going to go back to their own lives.

I go back home. My wife says, 'You okay? It's a lot. The girls don't live here anymore. Sundays you feel it the most, don't you? I feel it…'

Mr Connector cuts her off.

'Well, that's not going to help me right now. I need to get into work mode. Get ready for tomorrow's show.'

Total disconnection from my wife. But I wasn't connecting either with what was happening in my body. The ache in my heart, the lump in my throat. So much constriction—holding it all in.

Then she says, 'Chris, what code are you speaking?'

She cuts right through my bullshit. I start stuttering: 'No, no, no. I just need to focus'.

I doubled-down on the disconnection. 'I just need to focus on tomorrow's show.'

She goes, 'Right. Tell you what: I'll go make dinner in the kitchen. When Chris, my open-hearted husband, comes back online, send him into the kitchen for a chat'.

Wow. She's in connection, I'm in CODE.

Should I even be writing a book about the art of connecting?

Here's what I know to be true from my 28 years in radio.

Where you're speaking from is way more important than what you're saying.

Most speaking training focuses on the external: your body language, your vocal variety, your hand gestures, your slide design. All techniques. All mechanical.

But that's not where connection lives.

Connection lives in your state of being. In your presence. In whether you're actually here with the person you're talking to, or whether you're performing, managing or controlling.

It's not a technique. It's a state of mind that creates the conditions for genuine connection to occur. It's like the soil.

Please don't think this is some new hack to apply. Because people can feel the difference between someone using a technique and someone actually being present.

The magic of connection is that it allows all of us to be more in our truth. To feel more alive. To access more of who we actually are. Our fullness.

That's what we all want, isn't it?

Unfolders

Feeling into these questions, giving yourself time to sit with them, is more important than racing to an answer.

1. Where in your life could you turn up the connection dial by 10 per cent?
2. What are you trading connection for right now? What's the 'After I ______, then I'll ______' you're telling yourself?
3. What are you feeling right now that you're not letting yourself fully feel?

PART II
Tuning in

5

My toilet epiphany

Why do so many of life's breakthroughs happen when you're at your messiest? I don't mean on a nice meditation retreat or with a guru clearing out your chakras. I mean in the mud. In the chaos. In the panic.

For me, it came in the least glamorous place you could imagine: the men's toilet of an Australian radio station, at 6.03 am, with a little bit of sick down my shirt and my life falling apart.

Cubicle crucible

The mud was 2018. We'd just moved to Melbourne: me, Sarah, our girls and the dog. Ten days after landing, I launched a new breakfast show, and the city greeted me with a very Australian form of hospitality: a tidal wave of 'no' to some unknown English bloke on their radio.

But all that abuse was nothing compared to what came next.

Sarah was talking to her mum, Jackie, back in the UK one Tuesday evening when Jackie collapsed mid-call. Massive heart attack. We'd been in Australia for only a few weeks. Within hours I had to put Sarah and the girls on a plane back to London, not knowing if Jackie would be alive when they landed.

Minutes before the next morning's show, a call came from Dubai on their stopover. Through tears, Sarah told me the surgeons needed to operate on her mum for 11 hours. The odds weren't good. She'd been told to say her goodbyes, just in case.

This cannot be happening.

I felt trapped: stuck in a radio station nobody wanted to hear me on, away from my daughters who needed me, and terrified my second mum might die. Sarah—my rock—was sobbing in Dubai. Then I heard the 6AM news jingle fading and my own show intro blasting out of the ceiling speakers.

'Fuck,' I sighed.

Sarah, being Sarah, snapped back into Seal Team Leader mode: 'I can hear the show's starting! You've got to go, Chris. If Mum dies, I'm not moving back to the UK, so you need to dig in and make this work. I love you'.

I could hear the producers shouting for me. I yelled back, 'Play two songs back-to-back!' I needed time. I sprinted into the men's bathroom, kicked open a cubicle door and threw up. Dry heaving from fear and adrenaline. And the anticipation of more lovely messages from wellwishers.

Somewhere between the tiles and the dry heaves I remember asking myself, 'What are you going to do?' Not in the grand, heroic sense. Just... in the next three minutes.

I could feel the part of me that does live radio—usually accessible, usually game—was nowhere to be found. There was just noise. Fear. That old drill-sergeant voice in my head barking orders that didn't help.

And then an image arrived. Out of nowhere.

An old-fashioned radio tuner. A dial.

I could see it as clearly as I could see the cracked paint on the cubicle door. My internal dial was sitting firmly on *fear*. I imagined taking hold of it and nudging it a few clicks to the right. Again. And again. Off fear. Past anxiety. Towards something else.

Click, click, click... all the way to *joy*.

Joy. Yes, joy—ridiculous as that sounded in a bathroom with bile on my jeans.

As I pretended to turn that little dial, something in me actually moved. Unwound. My breath changed first. Then my jaw. And finally the smallest smile at the sheer cartoonishness of it all. My imagination being like a butler, serving me up a silver platter of salvation.

Choosing joy didn't erase the ache for Jackie, or the terror for Sarah. It didn't tidy anything up. It simply reminded me my heart could hold more than one thing at once. Grief and gratitude. Fear and a strange, quiet courage. Joy, even here.

We can be connected even to feeling disconnected. Just by being with it and allowing it. Our pain comes not from our feelings and emotions but from the resistance to them. Emotional fluidity is a super skill that I'm still trying to practise more.

I chose joy.

I wiped my face, met the team's worried eyes and started the show. I gave myself permission to enjoy doing what I love.

Jackie lived. Sarah and the girls returned weeks later. The road stayed bumpy.

But in that bathroom, I found something I still use every day—on air and everywhere else.

I found my inner dial.

(If you've ever had a spiritual awakening in a toilet, by the way, welcome to the club.)

The dial under pressure

Years later, the inner dial saved me again.

Middle of 2025. I got a phone call from Jack Post, my faithful sidekick on the radio show since I launched in Australia. We'd been through so much together. Built the show together. He'd tried to leave two years earlier, and I'd talked him into staying.

I was surprised. But also, not surprised when, one Wednesday afternoon, he called out of the blue with no prior warning and said his contract was coming to an end and he might be done. Obviously, not part of the plan—with the national show just around the corner in 2026.

It looked like he was going to leave. And leave in the next week!

I told him to take the rest of the week off. Just think about it. Until he'd made his decision, it'd be odd being in the studio together. He agreed and thanked me for the space.

Barely 12 hours later, I was in the studio before the start of the next show. My head was spinning. Where does this leave the show? How do I replace Jack? Is the show going to be good without him? What about the national launch?

I had to do my own work with this.

I had to use my inner dial.

I had to consciously shift my energy from fear and scarcity to abundance. I reminded myself that over my time in radio, I'd worked with many co-hosts and team members who'd come and gone. I've navigated these transitions many times before, sometimes with more grace than others.

And I literally remember thinking to myself—I'm not just saying this to sound edgy—*I give myself permission to enjoy the fuck out of today's show.*

Desperate times sometimes require an aggressive dial turn! And at 5.45 am, alone in a radio studio with a team looking into me from the other side of the studio window, like a human zoo, the heat was up really high in another crucible moment.

I'm spinning out. Worse, I can't share all this yet with the team. It's too much for them to process that and focus on the show right now.

I said to myself, *I am scared. And I love that.*

I allowed the fear in me to be met and loved. And then I said it again: *I'm going to enjoy the fuck out of today's show.*

That dial turn changed everything.

We had a phenomenal show. I really did enjoy the fuck out of it. And afterwards, I told the team everything. I also told them to enjoy the fuck out of this meeting. That bit made no sense, so I turned that dial back.

Buddha in the bathroom

The inner dial isn't denial. It isn't pretending you don't feel what you feel.

It's agency.

It's the moment you check where you're broadcasting from inside yourself, and choose—gently, with compassion—how you want to be.

Not what to say. How to *be.*

This discovery changed everything about how I speak and connect. It taught me that where you're coming from matters far more than what you're saying. We'll go deeper into this throughout the book: how you're actually a walking transmitter, how your frequency speaks louder than your words, how great conversation is really about two authentic signals meeting and amplifying each other.

But for now, just this.

Before your next conversation—the difficult one with your partner, the big presentation, the phone call you've been avoiding—give yourself a small gift.

Pause. Feel your feet. Check your inner dial. Pick an intention, how you want to be. Consciously shift your energy to your desired setting.

Where are you broadcasting from? Is that where you want to be?

Turn it, if you need to.

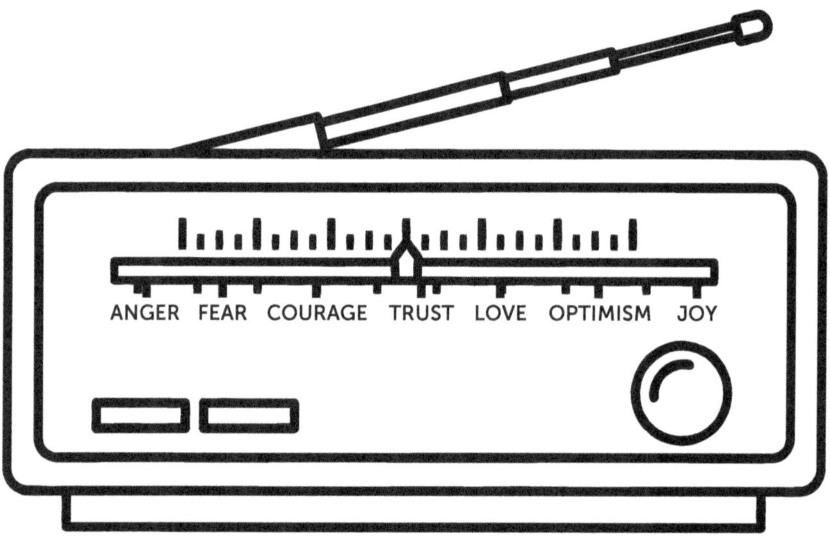

I've made a free, downloadable 'Inner Dial' visual tool/PDF, and guided audio meditation for the practice, at www.christianoconnell.com/unscript.

You don't have to be perfect. People don't want that; they really want to connect to you.

And if you forget? Remember this: even a toilet can be the place where you find your joy, your freedom and your frequency.

Unfolders

Three questions to sit with:

1. Think of a recent conversation that didn't land the way you wanted. Where was your inner dial tuned? Head (trying to fix, control, impress)? Gut (bracing, defensive, on alert)? Or somewhere else entirely?
2. When you're at your most connected with someone—really present, really with them—where does that come from in you? What does it feel like in your body?
3. Is there someone in your life right now who needs Real You instead of Superhero You? What would it take to sit on the floor with them?

6

The waves between us

One thing I'm known for in radio, alongside storytelling, is how I can connect very quickly and deeply with my callers.

This comes not from technique, or something to apply or do. It comes from opening my heart, presence and this compass: WAVES.

I'm sharing something I love using, being with, playing with. It's crystalised a way I've been having conversations for decades on air that can go deep and intimate very, very quickly. That can open up nervous callers, open up doorways and side doors in old stories listeners share that surprise them and us listening in turn.

It helped me disarm guarded celebrity guests in private jets (shout out to Chris Martin); in hotel rooms when I was about to walk out with a rude guest (shout out to major A-lister Superhero actor). It helped one of the biggest stars in the world drop his act and remove the sunglasses he was hiding behind at the start of our interview. It's really helped me interview hundreds of stars calling in live from somewhere in the world at zero notice during a big competition I've done several times called Who's Calling Christian?

Listeners could win a big cash prize by getting celebrities to call me live during the two weeks the game was being played. The celebrity would win the same big cash prize for the charity of their choice. Real edgy, exciting, unpredictable radio without any of the shock jock BS.

Highlights include Charlize Theron calling from a private jet on a runway in Berlin and the pilot, who listened to me, refusing to take off until she called me. Tom Hanks live from his film set, who then held up the scene being filmed yapping to me, so much so we just suddenly heard this angry voice yell out live on air from Tommy's set, 'We need to get *fucking moving!*'

But first, it was how I came to create a way of unifying my thoughts and principles into an easier system.

Melbourne, 2020. The longest lockdown in the world: 267 days. I'd moved to the most liveable city in the world, now the most locked down. It was unbearably hard on my daughters: teenagers stuck indoors trying to do online schooling. Doing my radio show was a salvation for me—and I hope for my audience. Barely a show went by without us getting calls from tearful listeners, struggling, but calling to say thank you for being there. I learned more about authentic connection during that time than in all of my previous years on air.

We could only travel within a five-kilometre radius of our homes. Five kilometres. That was it. That was your whole world for months.

And in those five kilometres? Luckily, I had two things that saved me: a public garden with some old oak trees, and the ocean.

It was the ocean that changed how I think about conversation.

I'm not a surfer, but I'd sit there watching the waves. My wife swam in the ocean daily. I preferred to sit on the beach and just be in awe of the waves. The rhythm resting me. And slowly—over those long, isolated months—I started to understand something about the dynamic nature of waves. How they're never the same twice. How they're shaped by forces under the surface you can't see. How they're both powerful and vulnerable, rising and falling, always in motion.

And I realised: conversations are like waves. All those years looking at soundwaves editing audio, the rise and falls, the falls and rise. It all felt connected.

What a wave actually is

I thought a wave was just what you see: that beautiful curl crashing on the beach. Done. Simple.

But that's not what a wave is at all.

A wave is a circular pattern of energy moving through water. That's what Sir David Attenborough taught me: the planet's actual teacher. If you slice a wave in half, the top part you see—that elegant curve, that curl—that's only half the story.

Most of the wave—the shape-maker, the force, the truth—is happening under the surface. Beneath what we can see. Circular patterns of energy, moving through the water, shaped by the ocean floor beneath it.

Shaped by what it meets.

Sometimes the shelf is steep, so the wave stands up tall, loud, sharp. Sometimes the floor is soft and shallow, so the wave rolls in gently, steadily, almost lazily. Sometimes there's a jagged reef underneath, so the wave curls fast, tight and aggressive.

The wave you see breaking is entirely shaped by what's happening in the depths you can't see.

And standing there watching wave after wave—no two the same, each one shaped by invisible forces—I realised: that's exactly what a conversation is.

We're never just listening to words

When two people talk, it's not just two brains sending data through the air like Bluetooth speakers. It's two bodies of water feeling each other's energy.

Swells. Pauses. Shifts. Eddies. Currents.

The words we say—the mood we're in, the tone we use—are just the surface. The curl. What you can see. But underneath? That's where all the real stuff lives.

Scripts we inherited. Stories we tell ourselves. Emotions we're pretending we're not having. Fear we won't name. History we're dragging behind us. The ache. The hope. The truth we're dancing around.

We're never just listening to words—we're listening to the shape of what's underneath the words.

When someone is defensive, you're seeing the surface. But beneath? Maybe they hit some old script or story that's frozen somewhere in them. This changes the shape of the energy moving through them, and that's why the soundwave is breaking rough. When someone's energy goes flat, something underneath has shifted. When the conversation suddenly catches fire, something deep has aligned. A surge of energy is moving through them and into you.

And here's what's wild: we are bodies of water. Somewhere between 55 and 60 per cent water. Which means we're not separate from the ocean of connection—we are part of it. Waves of energy don't just move between us—they move *through* us. Your emotions ripple through me. My state affects yours.

We're bodies of water in the same sea, already connected, with waves constantly moving between and through us.

Stories are waves too

There's fascinating research out of Princeton. Scientists recorded the brain activity of two people—one telling a story, one listening. What they found is that as the story unfolds, the listener's brainwaves start to synchronise with the storytellers. Not metaphorically. Literally. Their brain patterns mirror each other. The better the listener comprehends the story, the more closely the waves match.

The story isn't just heard. It's felt. It moves through the body. It creates resonance.

Isn't that incredible? It speaks to the primal power of stories as well.

This is why oral storytelling is so different from reading. When you read, you're alone with the text—the visual experience is analytic and individual. But when you hear a story? When someone's voice enters your ears and reverberates in your skull? You're not observing from a distance. You're in it. You are participating in it.

And this is exactly what used to happen around a campfire. The OG of shared experience and connection.

Someone starts telling a story. Their voice is rising and falling. Their hands gesture. Their eyes glint in the firelight. And everyone around the circle—their bodies start to synchronise. Breath patterns align. Attention focuses. The story creates a shared wave that moves through everybody present.

The same thing happens in conversation. When two people are truly connecting—not scripting, but authentically present, open, unguarded—their nervous systems entrain. Mirror neurons fire. Brainwaves sync. Breath patterns align.

You can *feel* when this happens. Time disappears. Words flow. You finish each other's sentences. It's what happens when you stop controlling and start surfing.

Scripts prevent synchronisation. When you're in your head—following the formula, worrying about what to say next—your brainwaves are doing their own thing. The other person's nervous system knows. Mirror neurons detect it. The wave crashes.

So, I started to understand my role on the radio show

Like a surfer.

Every morning, I wake up and prepare to surf. Not ocean wave — though the practice is the same. I'm getting ready to surf waves of sound, waves of energy, waves of human connection. When the show goes on air and the red *live* sign glows, I'll sit down with my co-hosts, open the phone lines and catch whatever waves the day brings. I'll meet the moment, what's here now.

Some mornings the conditions are perfect. The energy is flowing, the callers are alive, the conversation catches fire. We ride wave after wave of authentic connection. Stories, laughter, funny lines are created in the moment. It's like fireworks and sparks are coming through the speakers. We are the audience; the audience is us. Those are the mornings I live for.

Other mornings are choppy. The energy is different. My co-host is distracted. I'm tense. The topics aren't taking off like yesterday. On those mornings, I have to work harder to find the waves worth riding. Sometimes I'm just paddling out, reading the flows and patterns, waiting to catch something I can get up on and work with.

Sometimes I'm barely hanging on because the energy is so big.

But here's what I've learned after thousands of shows: you can't control the waves. You can't make callers be vulnerable. I can't push out of my heart some fear I'm holding about one of my daughters and what's going on in her life. We bring all of our messy selves to every interaction. I can't force a team member to be more present. You can't manufacture authentic connection through technique.

But you *can* learn to read the water. And work with it. You can sense what's happening beneath the surface. You can position yourself skilfully. You can manage the energy you're bringing. And you can ride what emerges with presence and skill—and even joy.

Jerry Seinfeld describes it like this: 'Stand-up for me is a surfboard. It's just you, you paddle out and you try and catch the energy and you're all on your own... That's how it feels when you're having a good set—like you've caught this gigantic energy and are just sliding down it'.

That's it exactly.

Every morning, I just paddle out. To meet the others, also paddling out with me.

Enjoyment over 'efforting'

A performance coach I know has worked with world champions and Olympic gold medal surfers. I asked him once how surfing competitions are scored. He said, 'Whoever looks like they're having the most fun, wins'.

That stopped me and lit me up. Sometimes just a single line can change how you see something.

We think it's about control, hard work, intense discipline. But the surfers who win aren't the ones grinding the hardest or following the most rigid technique. They're the ones gliding so effortlessly it looks like play. They make it play. We make our life harder than it needs to be.

That's how I want to live. That's how I want to speak. That's how I want to be in conversation with you, with the world, my family, with myself.

Most of your speaking is going to be in conversation

I love that word: conversational. It's active, has an energy to it. It even sounds like what it means, doesn't it? Con-ver-sa-tion-al. There's a rolling rhythm to it, a back and forth. Because conversation — real conversation — is how we find each other. It's how we find ourselves.

But here's what I've noticed: we're losing our conversational muscle. Our thumbs are jacked from phone workouts, but our connective tissue is weakening.

These days, people tell me they're more socially anxious than ever. They say they fear small talk. (I think it's not really small talk they fear — it's an emotion underneath it, but we'll get to that.) We've downsized face-to-face conversation, shrunk phone calls to text messages, WhatsApp threads, voice notes. We can record and re-record until they sound just right.

That's not a conversation. That's not speaking. That's editing yourself into existence.

Curated. Controlled. Safe. Dead.

Connect vs disconnect

There are two ways to approach a conversation.

- *The scripted way:* 'How much can I do *to* this conversation? How can I control, manage, manipulate? How can I steer it where I want, to get what I need out of it?'
- *The WAVES way:* 'How can I participate *with* what's emerging? How can I stay open instead of rushing to judgement? How can I be here instead of in my head?'

Think about it: a way to be with the ocean, riding a river—listening deeply to it and riding with its natural ebbs and flows. You might paddle every once in a while, but mostly it's a dance with the current, allowing things to unfold naturally. There's a deep effortlessness that arises from this way of being, and it's a lot more enjoyable, not to mention effective.

Now read that back and replace the word 'ocean' with 'conversation'. Same thing.

You can't surf a wave while you're stiff. You need a limber, flexible core—hips moving, knees bending, body responding to what the wave does. Surfers are in conversation with the ocean.

You can't connect while rigid—defended, controlling, tight. You need a regulated nervous system, an open body and a flexible response.

Scripts make you stiff. WAVES makes you limber.

In 2023, I did a three-month intensive masterclass with Joe Hudson, one of the world's most sought-after coaches to CEOs and leaders. He has a framework called VIEW: Vulnerability, Impartiality, Empathy, Wonder. It opened something in me.

But sitting with it afterwards, I needed to create my own version—one that came from my experience, my radio work, my body. Three letters overlap; the rest is mine. WAVES is what emerged from the ocean, and from the lab my radio studio has been at times.

So, this is where WAVES comes in.

It's not a technique. It's not a script. It's a way of being in conversation—a way of being in the ocean of 'us' together.

- *Wonder.* The engine driving it all.
- *Attunement.* How you tune into yourself affects how you tune into others.
- *Vulnerability.* Share what's in your heart. Even when it's uncomfortable.

- *Enjoyment.* Your state is your contribution to every conversation.
- *Surf.* Play. Remember how?

Each one gets its own chapter. Each one changed and changes how I show up.

I've made an easy-to-use, free, one-page downloadable document for WAVES at www.christianoconnell.com/unscript

WAVES is what I use during every single radio show. It's a compass I created because the map and territory, like the ocean, change every day. When I lose sight of the horizon, or the shore, it navigates me back to where I want to be—in my heart.

In chapters 7 to 11, I'll unpack the five components of my WAVES framework.

Unfolders

Three questions to sit with:

1. Think about your last really good conversation—one where time disappeared and you both left feeling more alive. What was happening beneath the surface? What invisible forces shaped that wave?
2. What do you think makes a great conversation?
3. 'Whoever looks like they're having the most fun, wins.' Where are you making conversation harder than it needs to be? What would enjoying it more actually look like?

7

Wonder

When did you stop being curious about people? Genuinely curious. Not polite-question curious. Not networking curious. I mean the kind of curious you were as a kid when you'd ask a stranger in the supermarket what they were having for dinner.

Somewhere between childhood and your first performance review, wonder got replaced by something else.

Let's look at having conversations from a place of wonder. This is the opposite of how many conversations are conducted, which is often about knowing, or more importantly, being seen as knowing.

Our desperate need to impress upon other people that we are smart and knowledgeable blocks genuine connection. We interact from our heads, our brains, trying to impress the other brains. It stops us listening, being fully present.

The way I see wonder is that it's blended with awe and curiosity. I think it's the most beautiful way of opening more fully to people and life. So much of our way of being is about knowing: knowing what you should say next, knowing what the person opposite you should do. We are conditioned at school to know the right answer, to feel shame if we are wrong. This is then carried with us into our adult lives.

The operating condition for my radio show is wonder. I'm never rushing to find an answer; I'm enjoying the ride along the way. Being in the question is way more enjoyable. What do we do once we find answers in life anyway? Throw them away and rush to another question we have to know the answer to.

Wonder invites you to move beyond that. This isn't some esoteric quality—it's an incredibly rewarding, magical and practical way to connect deeper and easier. It allows conversations to be more productive, totally transforms your problem solving and has huge benefits for your physical and mental health.

And this isn't just feel-good talk. Dacher Keltner's research at UC Berkeley found that those who experienced more awe had the lowest levels of inflammation in the body. Of all the positive emotions they studied, awe was the strongest predictor of better health. As Keltner puts it: 'The things we do to experience these emotions—a walk in nature, losing oneself in music, beholding art—has a direct influence upon health and life expectancy'.

Wonder is the engine driving it all. The fuel for all my creative output is wonder, curiosity and awe.

One of the most frequently asked questions I get is, 'Don't you worry about what you're going to talk about on air? Three hours a day, five days a week—don't you get scared about running out of things to say?'

Never. I worry about other things. But never that.

Wonder why?

If you live in wonder, there is no finite endpoint to it. There is no end destination.

Your curiosity and desire to be awed every day—that's a way of abundance. Not scarcity. This is allowing, receiving and listening. No striving needed. That's where I get my ideas from. Being in wonder about what I didn't know, what I might learn, what I might see. It's such a happier way to be.

Keltner identified eight wonders of life: moral beauty, collective effervescence, nature, music, visual design, spirituality and religion, life and death, and epiphany. Each one feels like being reminded of what's so wonderful about being alive. There's so much anger, fear, division and cruelty in the world that it's vital we remember the wonder and awe available around us, just waiting to be experienced. Of Keltner's eight wonders, here are a few that really lit me up with my own experiences of being in wonder and being awed.

Moral beauty

This is the awe we feel when we witness extraordinary goodness in another human being. I have the greatest example of this. On my show I was asking for stories of coincidence and chance. I got one of the most powerful emails and stories of all time. It always chokes me up when I read it…

It was from a listener named Paul and I'm going to let him tell it.

> Back in 1994 I was riding my motorcycle near High Beach in the UK. I was having a great day when all of a sudden I found myself upside down in a hedge and watching a plume of blood gush from my femoral artery. A few seconds later a fellow biker jumped on top of me and shoved his elbow hard into my groin. This stopped the blood and saved my life—I probably only had a few minutes left to live.
>
> This man was called Tom and was a retired army medic. After a short while, an ambulance arrived and I was saved. Tom and I became friends and he convinced me that everyone should have medical training, so I became a First Person on Scene responder.
>
> Well, time moved on. I had a family and moved away and gave up the bike and as such, Tom and I lost touch.

> This brings us to 2015. I was walking along the River Lee in Broxbourne and I heard screaming. A young girl had fallen in and gone under. I arrived as she was being pulled out and she wasn't breathing. With the help of another chap we gave her CPR and kept her going until the real medics arrived. This lovely young lady responded well to adrenaline and shock and came back to us.
>
> Before she left in the ambulance, her grandmother asked for my number so she could let me know how things went. After a few weeks, I got the call—Marie had made a full recovery and wanted me to come round for tea to say thanks.
>
> On arrival at the house I was met with big hugs and then I saw a picture on the mantelpiece. There was Tom with Marie on his knee, smiling at me.
>
> Marie was Tom's granddaughter.
>
> If Tom had not saved my life, not badgered me into learning first aid, I would not have been able to help his granddaughter. Tom passed away in 2014, so in a way, because of his actions, it was he who saved his granddaughter.

It's a beautiful story that shifts you into an open-hearted state of awe.

Tom never knew. He died a year before Marie fell into that river. He never got to see the circle close. The good he put into the world in 1994—stopping for a stranger, pressing his elbow into a wound, then badgering that stranger to learn first aid—just kept travelling. Through time. Through Paul. Until it found its way back to the person Tom loved most.

That's moral beauty. Not just witnessing goodness, but taking the time to slow down and really feel it. To bathe in its loving glow.

Paul put it better than I ever could:

If we live our lives with love, it will be returned to us.

Collective effervescence

This is the awe of moving together. From our separateness, to oneness. In community, having a shared experience, in communion.

You've felt it maybe singing with thousands of strangers. The roar of a stadium when your team scores. Going to the cinema and all responding as one with laughter or triumphant applause.

When I turned 50, I went to Western Ireland. Before embarking on a walking tour with 25 strangers from all over the world, led by the poet and philosopher David Whyte, I met my best friend Jamie in Dublin.

We went to see Bruce Springsteen.

Now, I'm a big Springsteen fan. My mum got me into Bruce, dancing around our tiny little front room to her vinyl copy of *Born in the USA*.

So there I was in Dublin. A Friday night — an uncharacteristically sunny Friday night in Ireland. The show was incredible. People of all ages — that's the power of The Boss.

Two things about that night speak of awe, wonder and collective effervescence.

The first: Springsteen said during the show, 'Thank you for being my purpose'.

It still gives me goosebumps.

Not *giving* me my purpose. *Being* my purpose. He saw no distinction between the music and us — the people. It was all purpose. All one thing.

The second thing happened as we left.

I've been to hundreds of gigs. You know what it's like leaving a great show — there's a buzz, an electricity. People are lit up. They want to go out, continue the night, make plans, talk about dreams, get drunk. They don't want it to end.

But this was different.

More than 20 000 people shuffled out in silence.

Not disappointed in silence. Not tired silence. Reverential silence. Like we were leaving a mass. Everyone in quiet contemplation of what we'd just experienced. Three hours of incredible rock and roll, and we walked out like we'd witnessed something holy.

I've never seen or felt anything like it.

That's the thing about collective effervescence—we think it's only the electric version. The buzzing, bouncing, screaming-along version. But sometimes it's this. The hush that falls over a crowd when they've touched something together that words can't hold.

Nature

This one seems obvious, right? Grand Canyon. Northern Lights. Great Ocean Road. Vast ocean vistas.

But nature doesn't require travel. It requires presence.

One day on my walking tour in Ireland, David and I stopped to marvel at a view of a huge valley and he said, 'Nature reminds us to leave ourselves alone, just to be unutterably ourselves'.

Do you remember the first time you felt—maybe you wouldn't have known the word for it then—something magical? You first felt awe. Some feeling in the body of light and wonder? Whether it was looking up at the moon, or standing at the edge of the ocean, whatever it was for you.

For me, it was a bird.

Now I'm going to share something with you here. If you thought the tree nerd was something, get ready to meet my other alter ego from childhood. Bless me: bird nerd.

You heard right. Bird nerd. Yes, I had my own binoculars as a young lad at seven and eight. I loved bird watching.

Don't put the book down. Please stay with me on this bird nerd journey.

The first time I ever experienced awe was when I saw an English bird called a Kingfisher. A Kingfisher has this iridescent orange chest and these blue, turquoise, royal blue wings. It is a magical-looking bird.

Those colours on the Kingfisher—when I saw it in the wild, sitting on a branch on a riverbank near my home—that was the first time I felt awe. I'd never seen anything like it. The colours did something to me internally. I can still feel it now. It's still working its magic on me.

I remember being curious and a bit upset that I'd never see it again, never experience it again. I remember scrunching my eyes up, trying harder to re-visualise it, to hold onto it—and I couldn't.

It was experiential. You can't think your way back to awe. You have to be there.

When I went back home recently to see my mum and dad in England, I was down in the countryside sitting in the garden by a riverbank with my mum at the Airbnb cottage I'd hired. And a Kingfisher appeared. Just for a moment. Then it flew off.

It put me straight back into awe. Forty-something years collapsed into nothing. Same bird. Same feeling. Same seven-year-old boy somewhere inside me, watching with his mouth open.

I think to this day I'm still looking for that Kingfisher—the Kingfisherness of the world.

Music

Music is a doorway. Into something. Into ourselves. Into our past, our present, our future. It helps us feel, immediately.

Music has been a way I bond with both my daughters. We'd just go for drives. Before they could drive themselves, they'd have my phone. And I miss these times so much. I yearn for them.

We'd go for these drives, just driving around. They'd play me a song—something they liked, something I'd never heard of. We'd talk about it. I'd pick a song. We'd talk about that. Then they'd pick one.

The music opened up parts of us. We'd have the funniest, most interesting, most joyous conversations. The words were just words. The music worked its magic underneath.

I miss those trips so much.

We went to all kinds of places. All in the front seat of the car.

Music helps us make sense of ourselves. It lifts us up. It lets us feel our pain, our joy. It's a time-travelling device—play a song from 10, 20, 30 years ago and watch what happens to you.

When I was 18, my best friends went travelling around the United States. I didn't have the money to go with them. I was heartbroken. Working in a factory for a summer job, six weeks, just to earn something. I was so depressed.

I remember being in my tiny bedroom, listening to the radio one night, feeling sorry for myself. And I heard them raving about some new band from Manchester called Oasis. They played a song called 'Live Forever'.

And that song lifted me out of that bedroom and into the possibility of who I might be, who I might become and what I could do.

It literally melted the walls of my bedroom.

To me, Oasis—and you'll have a band like this in your life, I hope—capture that time when you're 18, 19 and everything seems aflame. Aflame with potential. The world actually was just out there, waiting for you to get into it.

I was listening to an interview with the great Irish philosopher and poet John O'Donohue on Krista Tippett's podcast *On Being.* And he said something I'd never heard anyone say—one line that just summarised what music is:

Music is what language aspires to be.

Let that in.

Music is what language aspires to be.

Spirituality and religion

This isn't about belief. It's about experience.

Rob Bell points out that there's no word for 'spiritual' in the Hebrew scriptures. Because to call something spiritual would be to imply that other things aren't.

He tells the story of Moses and the burning bush. Moses doesn't take his sandals off because the ground suddenly becomes holy. The ground had been holy the whole time. The story is about Moses becoming aware of it.

That's what spiritual means. Not a separate category. Just... waking up to what's already there.

I had one of those wake-up moments in Ireland.

One day we hiked on the Burren, this extraordinary landscape of exposed limestone in the west of Ireland.

David Whyte led us down into a valley where we came upon a 2000-year-old stone fort. At one point, David unearthed from his cloth sack a bottle of Irish whisky. One of his assistants produced tiny plastic glasses, and we all had a shot, toasting each other and the land we were standing on.

Eventually, we reached a mound—an ancient burial site. Beneath this earth lay the bodies of many ancestors of Ireland.

David invited us to lie down. He said a few words. Then he asked us to call out the names of ancestors who were no longer with us.

And we did.

I called out my Irish grandparents. Two uncles. My Irish comedian friend and mentor, Sean Hughes. I heard other names being shouted—people I didn't know. Strangers calling to their dead.

And then we lay in silence. On and around this ancient burial mound. Our backs pressed to the earth.

I felt the spirit of the land. This energy under and above me. The spirits of something. I don't have better words for it than that. I felt awe. I was awed. I felt the Kingfisherness of the world again.

That's spirituality. Not a doctrine. Not a set of rules. Just the moments when the veil thins and you feel yourself connected to something that was here long before you and will be here long after. Your story meets a bigger story.

Life and death

Life and death. The two greatest teachers we have.

I saw it with Jackie's death—my mother-in-law, the woman who welcomed me into her family, was gone suddenly. Amid all the unbearable loss for my wife and all of us, there was also something else present. Wonder. Mystery. The strange, disorienting awareness that we don't know where we come from and we don't know where we go to.

Death brings life closer to view. It reminds us we're not here that long.

Once, on my radio show, I was giving away billboards to listeners. What do you want to say to millions of people on a billboard? These billboards were all over the city and were digital—I could change the wording within 15 minutes and suddenly it would just go live. Hundreds of thousands of people would see it.

The first day, a woman called in. She wanted a personal message for her husband, Steve:

Steve, put the dishes into the dishwasher.

And then there was the Tracy moment. I still get emails about the Tracy moment. She wanted to put on the billboard:

Don't wait until you get sick to start living your life.

Tracy had been diagnosed with terminal cancer. And she'd found incredible deeper meaning in her life since the diagnosis. She'd become a volunteer advocate—someone the police call when they've arrested a person who might have a learning difficulty. They call up volunteers like Tracy at all hours of the day and night, and she'd come in and patiently, kindly explain to that person what was happening.

Tracy was dying. But she was living more fully than most people ever do.

Don't wait until you get sick to start living your life.

If you've ever spoken to anyone who knows they are dying, one thing they have is this incredible clarity. It's like they see everything. The rawness. The sweetness. The vibrancy.

And then there's the other teacher. Birth.

I consider myself very lucky to have been there at the birth of both my daughters. Nothing will ever give me a greater sense of wonder and awe than that. Nothing. I've lived a life of adventure, of incredible wild excitement. But nothing will ever come close to seeing my daughters being born. Meeting Ruby. Meeting Lois.

Being floored just witnessing the divine power in my wife Sarah giving birth, having grown life in her and now releasing it into the world.

Both of the girls, as babies, were pure expressions of luminous, radiant beings of light. It took my breath away.

When I spoke earlier about looking for the Kingfisher—the Kingfisherness of the world, that iridescent flash of colour that stops you cold—that's what seeing my daughters emerge into the world was like. A miracle. Witnessing something truly wondrous.

Life emerging.

Epiphany

The word *epiphany* comes from Greek and means 'manifestation' or 'appearance'. Something that was always there, suddenly becoming visible.

The truth is always there. We're just not always able to see it. An epiphany isn't something arriving from outside—it's our eyes finally opening to what was present all along.

Lois, my younger daughter, and I used to love cycling to the woods near our house in the UK where she grew up. We found this tree with the lowest, thickest limb about a foot off the ground. We'd prop our bikes up by it and sit on that limb—it was like an extension of the tree, made for us. We'd fill a thermos with hot chocolate and bring some biscuits. We called it the Happy Hideaway. We even carved the initials HH into the trunk.

There's so much pressure on parents to create moments and memories with their kids, often thinking it requires spending a lot of money. I remember spending a small fortune taking the girls to Disneyland. They were wild with excitement about going to the Magic Kingdom. Hell, I was too. But when I asked them about that trip years later, they only remembered getting up very early and their mum being told off by a Disneyland employee for running between rides to beat the queues.

Lois holds that tree, the hot chocolate and the biscuits dear to her heart. Sometimes it sheltered us from rain. Other times it gave us shade from the sun. Just sitting there, enjoying hot chocolate, chomping on biscuits.

What's the epiphany? That there are no small moments. You can find a Magic Kingdom under a tree, drinking hot chocolate with your kid.

I felt it again when Ruby finished school, I planned a big trip for her to Queenstown, New Zealand. I spent ages booking incredible experiences: overnight river cruises, speedboat trips through gorges. But she got really ill a day before we left, so we couldn't do most of it. We spent a lot of time indoors, playing Scrabble and watching TV.

At the end of the trip, I apologised to Ruby for not giving her the trip she deserved. She said she'd actually had the best time. When I asked her for the highlight, she said playing Scrabble. Specifically, rude Scrabble one night. You get it. It doesn't need explaining.

The same epiphany. There are no small moments. When we take the time to be more present, from a place of wonder, we see and feel so much more.

The Magic Kingdom was never in Florida. It was wherever we stopped trying to create the moment and were actually fully present enough to enjoy what's here right now.

Wonder in action

One day, I was driving home after the radio show when I spotted a fire engine pulled over on the side of the road. Firefighters had a big ladder propped against a tree, and they were trying to coax a cat down from the upper branches. I pulled over to watch.

I got chatting to one of the firefighters, and I said to him, 'I thought this only happened in movies and sitcoms'.

He laughed. 'No, no, no. You'd be surprised how often we get called out for this.'

That conversation sparked something. The next day on air, I asked listeners: 'Have you ever called triple-0, the emergency services, for a non-life-threatening reason?'

The calls we got were incredible.

One old man had gotten stuck on a lawn chair that was in his shower. Because of his age, his testicles had descended through the slats in the chair, and when he tried to stand up, the chair came with him. The shower had gone cold and everything had, well ... you get the idea.

But my favourite call was from a woman who'd rung the fire brigade to rescue her cat from a tree. While the firefighters were setting up their ladder, the cat casually climbed down on its own. But in the process of trying to rescue the cat, one of the firefighters had gotten stuck in the tree. So she had to call the fire brigade again and say, 'No, no, the cat's fine. But one of your guys is now stuck in the tree. Can you come and rescue him?'

That's what wonder gives you.

Ashes, crocodiles and chicken rissoles

For a brief time, I tried to learn golf. The guy teaching me was funny, and among the coaching we talked about life and family. I discovered his wife had died two years ago. He said he had a funny story about her ashes.

He did.

He and his sons went on their favourite walk to a cliff top where they loved the view. They said a few words, played her favourite song and tossed the ashes into the air.

Like any good storyteller, he paused for effect.

'The wind direction ... Christian, it changed really dramatically.'

She blew back onto his face. Coughing and spluttering. His sons started laughing and pointing at dad covered in ashes. How wonderful it must have been for them all to share a laugh in that hard moment.

So I asked for stories on air. 'What did you do with the ashes?'

Because I was being in wonder, I thought we might get a couple of calls. We got so many calls we did five shows on it. The entire week.

The one that will always remain with me was the woman who said her dad loved crocodiles. He loved this big state park where there were crocodiles, and she said, 'We fed Dad to the crocodiles'.

'What do you mean, "fed him"? His ashes?'

'Yeah, yeah, yeah. Fed his ashes.'

'But how? You can't just go and sprinkle it—it might get in the crocodile's eyes and then they go for you.'

She said they'd looked online and found a recipe for chicken rissoles, then mixed the ashes into the chicken rissoles and fed those to wild crocodiles. They'd found someone to take them into the state park at night, where they knew crocodiles were.

Chicken rissoles. With ashes. For crocodiles.

That's what wonder creates.

72-hour groundhog day

A few years ago, I introduced my daughters to the movie *Groundhog Day*. At the end of it, I was thinking: how many times could you watch that movie without going crazy?

Hang on. I could turn that into a competition.

So I created the 72-Hour Movie Marathon: *Groundhog Day* played continuously for 72 hours. The last person standing wins $10 000.

Something amazing happened. We thought one person would win. They'd drop out one by one. But they stopped competing against each other. In the end, as it got really hard in the last few hours, they sat arm in arm, linked up on the floor of the cinema, keeping each other awake. Because if you fell asleep, you were out. They started out as strangers and then bonded through this insane experience.

We had to share the $10 000 among several winners.

That's what wonder can create. Not just ideas, but moments where people surprise themselves, where they remember we belong to each other.

The person in front of you *is* the wonder

Keltner's research asked people from 26 countries, 'What most commonly led you to feel awe? Was it nature? Spiritual practice? Music?'

The answer: 'In fact, it was *other people's courage, kindness, strength or overcoming*.'

The person in front of you *is* the wonder.

Their story, their survival, their truth—that's what creates awe.

Everyday magic

Not long ago, a listener called Shelley rang in with a story. She'd had a mixed-up day and ended up at the wrong Bunnings—not her local one. At the counter, the woman serving her picked something up off the floor and said, 'You've dropped your licence'. Then she turned it over. 'Oh, it's not you anyway. It's a man.' She looked closer. 'Oh, he's from Crib Point.'

Shelley froze. 'Five Point Road?'

The woman nodded yes.

Shelley burst into tears. That was her family home. Her father had lived there for 50 years before he died. It wasn't the stranger's local Bunnings. It wasn't Shelley's local Bunnings. Two mixed-up days. One dropped licence. One address read aloud by a woman behind a counter. A sliding door moment—literally, the automatic doors of a Bunnings.

An employee came to the counter with the power tool that Shelley had wanted to exchange and found her in tears. He said, 'It's all right, love. You're going to get it replaced. We're going to sort that DeWalt out'. He thought she was crying about the power tool.

Shelley returned the licence to the stranger. He wasn't home when she went by, but she dropped by the next day. They talked for 45 minutes.

He's from England. She told him he had an adopted family now. He's coming up for a barbecue.

I asked Shelley on air: 'Did you feel your dad's presence?'

She went quiet for a moment. Then she said, 'Yes. We were a very close family'.

That's wonder. Not planned. I was following my curiosity. Not scripted.

But here's what I didn't know.

Two weeks later, I received an email from a woman called Meghanne. She told me that her partner had been diagnosed with a rare form of cancer that year. They have two kids—a five-year-old and a seven-year-old. He had spent most of the year in hospital before passing away in September.

She'd been listening to Shelley's call in the car with her daughter. And when I asked Shelley, 'Did you feel your dad's presence?' and Shelley said yes, her seven-year-old daughter heard it.

And she started talking to her mum.

About her dad. The dad who'd just died. About whether we can still feel people after they're gone. About presence and absence and love that doesn't end.

A question I asked a stranger about a dropped licence in a hardware store opened up a conversation between a grieving mother and her seven-year-old daughter about life and death and whether the people we lose are still with us somehow.

Meghanne wrote: *Your show was a constant form of connection for us as a family when we didn't even know we were needing it in those moments.*

And then she wrote this line, which I will never forget:

Thank you all for helping us laugh when we didn't know if we'd be able to.

That's the thing about wonder. You never see where it goes. You stay curious. You ask the question that wants to be asked. You pull the thread.

Shelley's story touched moral beauty, spirituality, life and death—three of Keltner's eight wonders, all sparked by a mixed-up day and a dropped licence. And it rippled outward in ways none of us could have predicted.

Wonder isn't just a method for having better conversations. It's a way of living and being in this world.

Wonder is how we come alive.

Unfolders

Three questions to ponder:

1. When was the first time you can remember feeling awed?
2. When was the last time?
3. What would need to change to open more of your day-to-day life to wonder, awe and curiosity?

8

Attunement

Attunement.

It's not just about connecting better—it's about what we lose when we forget we're human.

A is for *attune*.

When a conversation dies, and they just do sometimes, it's often because no-one acknowledges it because we mostly run on autopilot in our interactions. We are overwhelmed and time starved. Distracted and up in our heads. But when we remember to take the smallest amount of time to *attune*, our conversations come alive with life, and us. Both parties leave lit up.

This word though: attune. What does it mean? Let's break it apart and something beautiful emerges.

At + Tune.

To bring yourself *to tune* with something. To tune *towards*.

And 'tune' comes from 'tone'—from the Greek *tonos*, meaning the pitch of a voice, the tension in a string that creates sound. Attunement is literally about finding the same frequency. Adjusting yourself until you resonate with what's in front of you.

For me, it's even simpler: *Attention + Tune.*

Where is your attention tuned right now?

I've spent almost 30 years in radio, tuning into people. Finding their frequency. When there's static, I adjust. When I'm in tune with a caller, everything flows. Tuning isn't forcing. When you tune a guitar, you don't wrestle the string into submission. You adjust, listen, adjust again. Small movements until it resonates.

That's attunement. You're not forcing connection. You're adjusting yourself until you find the shared note.

If wonder opens your eyes to what else might be true, attunement opens your whole self to who is actually here. Present.

The river

In wonder, nature taught us through oak trees and birds. Now nature has another teacher for us: rivers.

I love rivers. At the bottom of the road from the house where I spent the first eight years of my life was the River Itchen—a beautiful chalk stream flowing for 60 kilometres, internationally protected, home to Kingfishers and otters. Most days I'd be down by that water, hypnotically calmed by its rushing sound, which I could even hear from my bedroom at night.

Rivers don't force. They flow. They find their path around obstacles. They're always the same river but never the same water. And they teach us something profound about connection.

Imagine putting your hand into a river. If you move your hand at exactly the speed of the water—matching its flow, its rhythm, its direction—you feel no pressure at all. Your hand becomes part of the river. But the moment you push against the current, or drag behind it, you feel resistance.

That's attunement. Matching the flow.

And that pressure we feel in so many conversations? That tension, that sense of pushing or being pushed? That's what happens when we're not attuned. We're fighting the current instead of joining it.

Attunement is the art of tuning in—to yourself, to others and to the space between you. It's deeper than listening. It's sensing. Feeling. Tracking. It's what happens when two nervous systems recognise each other and start to flow together.

Think of it like riding a bike beside someone on their bike (neither of you is wearing Lycra.) When you're paddling at the same speed, conversation is easy. You can talk, laugh and share. But the moment one of you speeds up or slows down, communication gets harder. You're shouting over the gap. You're out of sync. Someone is getting left behind.

You can exchange words perfectly and feel absolutely nothing. Or you can stumble through something awkwardly and walk away changed. The difference isn't the words. It's whether you were actually *there*. Whether you were tuned in. Whether you found the shared flow.

Why does it matter? Because without attunement, you're not having a conversation—you're having two intersecting monologues in the same room. You're talking *at* someone, not *with* them. You might hear their words, but you'll miss their meaning. You'll see their face, but you'll miss their heart.

Attunement is how we find each other beneath the noise and static, and there are two ways we can do this.

The machine frequency

We're always attuned to something. The question is *what*.

Right now, our world is tuned to what I call the Machine Frequency.

Have you noticed the language we use about ourselves? We talk about 'optimising' our mornings. 'Hacking' our sleep. Being '10× more productive.' We track our steps, our heart rate variability, our deep sleep cycles. We measure our worth in output. We've downloaded apps to tell us when we're stressed, as if our bodies were unreliable narrators of our own experience.

We've given away and outsourced our own knowing, power and authority.

Listen to how we talk about each other: 'I don't have the bandwidth for that'. 'Let me download you on what happened.' 'I need to recharge.' We've absorbed the language of technology so completely we don't even notice it anymore.

We call these KP fucking Is!

My only KPI as a leader is connection.

Here's what happens when we tune to the Machine Frequency: we flatten ourselves. We forget how wide and deep and mysterious it is to be a human being. We start treating ourselves as things—objects to optimise, systems to debug, problems to solve.

And when we relate to ourselves as objects, we do the same to everyone else. We reduce them to objects in our own image. Resources. Headcount. Obstacles. Means to an end.

It's this flattening—of ourselves and each other—that attunement undoes.

It's making us more divided.

But it's worse than lonely. It's dangerous.

Because a machine is an object. An object is a thing. And things don't have feelings. Things don't have histories or hopes or childhood wounds or hearts that break. Things don't deserve compassion. Things can be discarded.

I think we've slid into seeing each other—and maybe ourselves—as things. Things. Stripping away our depth, our mystery, our wonder, our hearts and souls, our weirdness, our gold.

This is how we've learned to treat each other online. And increasingly, in real life too. It's so much easier to dehumanise a thing. To dismiss it. Mock it. Destroy it. And feel nothing.

And here's what I've noticed: the cruelty we see in debates, the pile-ons, the righteous fury—none of that is possible when you're tuned to the Human Frequency. You can disagree with a human. You can argue passionately. But you can't hate them the same way. Not when you see them as a person with a heart that hopes and breaks, same as yours.

The Machine Frequency doesn't just disconnect us. It makes us capable of cruelty we'd never allow if we remembered who we were talking to.

The Human Frequency

But there's another frequency available to us.

The Human Frequency is tuning into what's real for its own sake. Not to fix it. Not to use it. Just to see it clearly and let that be enough.

The Human Frequency is noticing the barista is tired today. Not because it affects your coffee—but because she's a person and you saw her. It's loving what's true and beautiful, not because you'll gain anything from it, but because paying attention to those things is its own reward.

When we tune to the Human Frequency, we see an enchanted world, not a broken one. We notice beauty in faces, inherent worth in all beings. We sense the profound value of others—and ourselves. We sense our togetherness.

This isn't soft or impractical. It's actually more *accurate*. Because the person in front of you isn't a machine. They're not a resource to leverage or a problem to solve. They're a human being with a heart that hopes and breaks, with dreams and fears and a whole universe of experience you'll never fully know.

The invitation of attunement isn't to tune in to what's useful. It's to tune in to what's true. What's here right now. To be more authentic you need to be more present. Only when we are present can we be ourselves. You can't schedule authenticity for 10 am tomorrow morning!

So, let me ask you: What frequency is your attention tuned to today?

Beyond listening

We've all been taught about 'active listening'. Make eye contact. Nod. Reflect back what you heard. Ask follow-up questions. These are good skills. They're just not attunement.

Active listening hears information. Attunement feels truth.

I could be nodding, making eye contact, asking all the right questions, and still be completely absent. Still running my own internal monologue. Still waiting for my turn to speak. Performing 'good listening' without actually being present.

Here's something I've noticed after thousands of conversations on air: sometimes a conversation dies in the middle, and nobody notices. It just flatlines. Two people still talking, words still being exchanged, but the aliveness has left the room.

It's not really anyone's fault, and apportioning blame doesn't help. Autopilot is a mode most of us are in for most conversations. Let's forgive ourselves for that—life is overwhelming.

But here's the thing: a dead conversation can be reignited. When we take even the smallest moment to adjust—come back into wonder, attunement—life can return. I see it like there's always a light on in us. Like that pilot light in a boiler.

Or am I getting us back to being things?

Maybe. But I do find it helpful to see the light in all of us. If I don't, then what? And that inner light behind our eyes—the one that's never changed since we were born—we can use that. In me. In you. In the space between us. If we choose to.

And here's the cruel irony: often it's our very wish for the conversation to go well that kills it. Managing the whole thing can deaden with a heavier hand than is needed. We want it to land, so we reach for a technique. We want connection, so we deploy a method. And the moment we do, something real gets replaced by something performed.

The conversation doesn't die from neglect. It dies from trying too hard.

There's something beautifully sad about that, isn't there? I can think of so many examples where my intention was good, but my impact wasn't great.

When I'm truly attuned to a caller on my radio show, I'm tracking their words and I'm also tracking their emotion—what they're feeling beneath those words. Their energy. Their needs—what they're really asking for, which is often different from what they're saying.

I'm not just listening to what they're saying. I'm listening to what they're *not* saying. The catch in their voice. The pause that lasts a beat too long. The brightness that's trying too hard. The thing they're circling but won't land on.

The words are just the surface of the river. Underneath them—in the deeper current—that's where everything real lives.

Radio has taught me attunement because I only have voices to work with. By closing down one sense, the visual, the others get stronger. I'm not distracted by what I'm seeing. I can really fine tune—fine *attune*—on what's under the words.

The CEO who was really a dad

I was coaching a CEO whose armour was his job title. In our first session, he mentioned he was a CEO about 13 times. His LinkedIn was practically tattooed on his forehead.

He was speaking from his head, trying to impress my head with status and achievement. That's the Machine Frequency in action—two systems exchanging data about their relative positions.

But connection doesn't happen head-to-head. It happens heart-to-heart.

So I asked him about his son. And something shifted.

His voice cracked—just slightly. His armour split for a moment. Suddenly I wasn't sitting across from a CEO. I was with a dad. A human being who loved his son deeply and was terrified of failing him.

That's attunement. I wasn't listening to his title. I was listening for his truth. And when I asked about his son, I wasn't gathering information—I was creating an invitation. An invitation to drop the persona and show up as a person.

He accepted. And in that moment, two strangers became two humans actually meeting each other. A couple of dads speaking from the heart, not the head.

Here's the thing about personas I can say from my personal experience: they're exhausting to maintain. And underneath every polished presentation, there's a person who's tired of pretending and just wants to be seen and met.

Attunement sees them.

What happens when you drop the script

For Father's Day on the show, we asked people to call in and pick a song that reminds them of their dad.

One caller rang in wanting to hear 'Cotton-Eyed Joe' by the Rednex. Not a great song, let's be honest. But midway through the call, this lovely guy—David—suddenly said his dad had died a few years ago. The song always reminds him of his dad because he would get up after he'd had a few drinks and do this silly dance to 'Cotton-Eyed Joe'.

That's the moment. Right there. He dropped from being in script—in his head, recounting a funny anecdote—to sharing his heart. From performance to presence. From persona to person.

We played the song. And we got so many messages from people who'd found themselves in his story. Who'd shared a tear with David while listening to the Rednex at 10 past 8 on a Friday morning.

Who knew 'Cotton-Eyed Joe' could be so profound?

Here's what attunement taught me in that moment: I heard the shift *before* he said the sad part. His rhythm changed. His pace slowed. Something in the quality of his voice softened before the words caught up.

If I'd only been listening to his words, I would have stayed in 'funny story' mode. But because I was attuned to the whole of him—the frequency beneath the content—I felt the turn coming. I made space for it instead of filling it.

That's the difference between listening and attunement. Listening hears the words. Attunement feels the person.

You can't attune to others if you abandon yourself

I just want to make something clearer. Attunement isn't just focusing entirely on the other person. Merging with them. Losing yourself in their experience.

That's not attunement. That's collapse.

True attunement has three parts: Me connected to me. The space between us. And you. All three, held at once.

When you're not attuned to yourself, something else kicks in: overthinking. Here's the tell: *What you can't feel in life, you have to overthink.*

When you're not fully attuned to someone, your mind races: 'Did he really mean that?' 'What was she feeling?' 'Why did they say it that way?' That mental chatter isn't intelligence working harder. It's intelligence compensating for a felt sense that's gone offline.

Underthink. Attune to what's really alive and emerging right now.

When you feel someone clearly, you don't need to analyse them. When you're in the flow of the river together, you don't need to think about the current. You're in it.

I learned this the hard way early in my radio career. I thought being a good interviewer meant completely focusing on the other person. Preparing and researching smart questions to impress them with. Then not really hearing their answers, just in 'interviewer mode' and thinking about the next question. I'd lose myself in their story. I'd forget I was there. And you know what? Those interviews were flat. Something was missing. I wasn't bringing myself to the conversation. I was abandoning myself in the name of 'listening'. What also happened was they checked out and went into autopilot mode, regurgitating stock answers they'd said too many times.

To attune is to inhabit yourself fully and listen from your wholeness.

Me. The space between us. You. The whole river, not just their bank.

The *how* matters

Earlier in the book, I said that where you are coming from matters more than what you are saying.

This is all about that.

It's not just *that* you attune. It's *how* you attune.

If you attune with suspicion, you'll find evidence for suspicion. Attune with judgement? You'll find things to judge. Attune with an agenda? You'll only hear what serves it.

You can listen with a closed heart and from a place of anger. But you are technically listening.

Just notice the quality of your questions.

Most questions aren't questions at all. They're judgements dressed up in question marks.

'Why would you do *that*?' Translation: That was stupid.

'Don't you think you should … ?' Translation: I think you should.

'Have you considered … ?' Translation: You clearly haven't thought this through.

These aren't questions born from wonder. The other person feels it instantly—even if they can't name it. Their body tightens. Their walls go up. Connection dies.

When I ask a question with an agenda—even a subtle one, even a 'good' one like wanting to steer someone towards a heartwarming conclusion—something closes. They feel the invisible hand trying to move them somewhere. You're trying to steer the river.

The question might sound identical. But the frequency it's transmitted on changes everything.

Pub Epiphany

One day I saw it with utter clarity. Which is rare for me—I'm a slow clarity kind of guy.

I was at the Edinburgh Comedy Festival. This is the world's biggest comedy festival. For the month of August, the great Scottish city is like a giant clown convention. For three consecutive years I took new stand-up shows there and performed seven nights a week for the month! It was intense, brutal—worrying about sales, reviews, competing with the best comedians from all over the world. It was also brilliant. Like a boot camp for comics.

I was having lunch with a comedian playing a way bigger room than me. I was playing to hundreds, he to thousands. He was feeling good and telling me how much money he was making. I loved this guy. But right then, I was hating the fucker.

As we were talking, I noticed behind him in this pub was a big mirror. And I caught my reflection. The thing was, the mirror was cracked—so I was looking at a warped view of myself.

And right there, in a pub, feeling bitter and resentful, came my epiphany. I've had them in toilets. Now a pub. I saw it. I really did.

The hall of mirrors.

I wasn't seeing him and his well-earned success. I was filtering it all through me. My insecurity. My comparison. My story about what his success meant about my worth.

How much of our experience of another person is first about us? Our hopes. Our fears. Our filtering and interpreting. Our projections. And every experience they have of us is first about them.

We're all walking around in a hall of mirrors, thinking we're looking at each other when mostly we're looking at ourselves reflected back.

So the question becomes, 'What do we have to let go of to actually meet the person in front of us—instead of just meeting ourselves wearing their face?"

There's someone else in the conversation...

Here's where it gets even more interesting.

We don't just attune to the person in front of us. We attune to them *through* every significant relationship we've ever had.

We have ghost scripts running.

Your partner asks, 'How was your day?' and you sense they aren't really listening—suddenly you're not talking to your partner. You're talking to your mother, who never listened fully to you. So you get defensive. Or you shut down. Or you give a one-word answer to a question that deserved more.

Your boss gives you feedback and suddenly they're not your boss—they're your father, who only noticed you when you failed. So you can't hear the feedback. You can only hear the judgement you're projecting onto it.

We turn lovers into parents. Colleagues into siblings. Strangers into old enemies. And then we wonder why connection feels so hard.

We carry an attunement template—built over years, usually in childhood—and we unconsciously lie it over everyone we meet. We're not tuning into *them*. We're tuning into our projection of them, filtered through old pain, old patterns, old fears.

Here's something to play with. When you feel stuck or have some issue you're trying to get clear on, ask yourself, 'Who else is in this conversation?'

There may be a ghost script from Mum, Dad, a teacher like *Mrs Cat Shit Breath!*

These ghost scripts act like Vaseline over the lens of our connection.

Attunement doesn't fight the behaviour. It sees the feeling beneath it.

Beneath every behaviour there is a feeling. Beneath every feeling there is a need. When we meet that need rather than focus on the behaviour, we begin to deal with the cause, not the symptom.

Read that again. It's important.

Most conflicts escalate because we react to what's on the surface—the behaviour. They say something hurtful, we respond to the hurt. They withdraw, we respond to the withdrawal. They blame, we defend against the blame.

But the behaviour is never the real issue. It's just the visible part of the iceberg.

Anger? Usually there's hurt underneath. Distance? Usually fear. Withdrawal? Overwhelm? Blame? An unmet need they don't know how to express. Criticism? Often, a longing in disguise.

When you *attune to the feeling beneath the behaviour*—and the need beneath the feeling—everything shifts. You're no longer fighting. You're seeing.

When someone feels attuned to, conflicts can dissolve. Not because you've agreed with them. Not because you've fixed anything. But because they finally feel felt. And often, that's all they needed.

The scary part: Attuning to yourself

We've covered that attunement isn't just about connecting with others. It starts with connecting with yourself. And that can be uncomfortable sometimes. We're often strangers to ourselves.

Because when you truly tune in to yourself, you might discover things you've been avoiding. Grief you've been outrunning. Needs you've been denying. Desires that don't match your life. Truths that demand change.

If I start attuning to what's really true underneath, my whole life might change.

That's the threat. And the promise.

But here's the gift: attuning to yourself quiets the noise in your mind, so you can hear the quieter wants. Underneath the shoulds and the supposed-tos and the inherited goals, there's something more true. Your actual desires. Your real needs. What's true for you *now*, not what used to be true.

And intuition is a by-product of attunement to self. The more you tune into your own experience—your body, your feelings, your knowing—the more you can trust what you sense about others and about life.

Swimming in the river

Here's one more thing the river teaches us.

We often think of ourselves as separate from life—standing on the bank, watching the water go by, trying to figure out when to jump in. But we're not on the bank. We're already in the river. We always have been.

Life isn't something happening to us. It's something flowing through us. The question isn't whether to get wet—we're already wet. The question is whether we'll fight the current or find the flow.

Attunement is finding the flow.

Most of us were never taught this. We fumbled through conversations performing listening, leaving ourselves, reacting to surfaces, missing each other entirely. We stayed on the Machine Frequency because it was all we knew. We pushed against the river and wondered why everything felt like such hard work.

But it can be learned. The act of attuning increases attunement. Like tuning forks, people resonate. When you attune to someone, you model it for them. You give them an experience they might never have had. You show them what's possible.

And every conversation is practice. Every time you catch yourself on the Machine Frequency and choose the Human Frequency instead, you're rewiring decades of conditioning.

It won't be perfect. You'll drift back into your head. You'll catch yourself performing listening instead of actually listening. You'll realise you've been talking to your mother when the person in front of you is your wife.

That's okay. Come back. That's the practice. To attune means to retune. To return means to attune.

You have permission to stop optimising yourself. You have permission to be human—messy, inefficient, gloriously unquantifiable. And you have permission to see others that way too. Not as problems to solve or resources to leverage. As fellow humans, doing their best, hoping to be seen. As fellow swimmers in the same river.

Wonder asked, 'What else could be true here?'

Attunement asks, 'Who is really here—including me?'

Put your hand in the water. Match the current. Feel no pressure.

That's Attunement. That's where connection lives. That's what makes us human.

Unfolders

Three questions to sit with:

1. What frequency are you usually tuned to? Think about your typical conversations—at work, at home, with strangers. Are you attuning to people as resources to manage, problems to solve, systems to optimise? Or are you tuning into the human beneath the role—their hopes, their struggles, their essential goodness? What would shift if you changed frequencies?
2. Who are you really talking to? In your most charged relationships—with your partner, your parent, your boss, your child—who do you actually hear when they speak? Are you responding to them, or to a ghost from your past wearing their face? What old attunement template might you be laying over someone who deserves to be seen fresh?
3. Over the next few days, try this before your conversations. Take a moment to attune. For me, my breath is a way back to attuning to myself. Just three to five breaths; I like the 4–6 method. That's four seconds in gently, then a longer six-second outbreath. I take in the in breath through my nose, then exhale through my mouth slowly as if I was doing it through a straw. Feel your goodness, see it in the people you're about to speak to. See what happens now in your conversations. Enjoy.

9

Vulnerability

For any conversation where you want to show up authentically, you will need vulnerability.

Let me give you the whole chapter upfront:

You can't be authentic without being vulnerable, and you can't be vulnerable without being authentic. That inseparable pair is what I call your connectability—your capacity to connect at a deeper level.

Here's the question I keep coming back to: when life gets tight—and it does—do I close down or stay open? Do I withdraw into my fear or turn towards my courage, my self-compassion, and stay open-hearted to it all? Which way keeps me small? Which invites me into my fullness?

I dare to lead with heart and vulnerability. That's often scary, messy and uncomfortable, but it is the path of true transformation, connection and aliveness.

I'll do it right now.

Ghosting for grown-ups

I cancelled a speech about vulnerability because I wrote a book about vulnerability—because I was scared of being vulnerable.

A man named Daniel, who leads a Jewish men's group, emailed me after reading my book, *No One Listens to Your Dad's Show.* He asked me to come and give a talk about vulnerability. I said yes.

And then I stopped replying to his emails.

For a year and a half.

I just … ghosted him. Because I was worried I'd have a panic attack while talking about vulnerability in front of a room full of men. The irony wasn't lost on me. I'd written a book about this stuff, and I couldn't face talking about it.

After 18 months of silence, I finally rang Daniel. I said, 'I'm really sorry. I was feeling vulnerable about talking about vulnerability. And I'd love to come and do the talk if you still want me'.

He said he'd speak to his group. They'd vote on it.

They voted yes.

And that became the talk. You can be vulnerable about being vulnerable. That *is* the practice.

The talk was held in a community sports centre, in a room above a squash court. Fluorescent lights. Plastic chairs. This is where men go to talk about vulnerability.

The men shuffled in, apprehensive about me, about the topic, about what they might be asked to feel. For protection, many arrived clutching a bottle of beer to their chest—like a sword. Or a teddy bear.

And then came the introduction …

'Now, I know there has been some reluctance about tonight's speaker. Some of you expressed concerns as to why we invited him and what someone like him would have to say of any value … '

I nearly walked out.

A room full of men older than me by 10, 20, 30 years. Lawyers. Business owners. Accountants. Way more professionally accomplished than me. And apparently, some of them didn't even want me there. The last speaker was one of the most respected and successful sport coaches in Australia, and now it was a guy who played Nickelback for a living who didn't even want to be there.

Perfect conditions for a group of men to be vulnerable.

I told them the truth. That I'd ghosted their leader for 18 months because I was scared. That I'd written a book about vulnerability and still sometimes found it hard to be vulnerable. This gave me an authentic way to talk about the courage required for vulnerability. Why we resist it: because we are choosing to avoid feeling certain emotions.

The questions afterwards were incredible. One man cried talking about his disconnection from his daughter. 'I'm not good at this vulnerability stuff,' he shared, and was met with many nods of agreement.

You don't have to be good at it. Sometimes it comes out bumpy—like that garden tap when you first turn it on after it's not been used for a while. The water runs brown at first. But as it flows, it runs clearer. The more vulnerable you are, the better you can create a new story and kill an old script about what you can handle.

At the end, something beautiful happened. Daniel stood up and started a standing ovation. I have to say, I enjoyed the vulnerability ovation! Only 50 or so people there, in that room above the squash courts, and again I was shown—and they were shown—what vulnerability leads to. Deeper connection.

As I left, way after the talk ended because they now had so much to say, I was followed out like a pied piper as I walked to my car. My last image of this very special night was a 70-year-old urologist handing me his card saying, 'For 20 years' time, when you'll need it'.

What vulnerability actually looks like

This chapter isn't theory. It's not wisdom from a safe distance. It's me telling you what happened when I tried to live this stuff—and how messy, scary and also transformative it turned out to be. This is living at your edges, and that's where a freer, more expansive life is waiting.

One thing to say for clarity is that vulnerability isn't about the absence of fear. It's about holding fear in your heart. Loving fear. Allowing fear. Moving forward with it anyway.

Choosing love over fear. Or maybe more honestly: choosing love *with* fear.

The book that changed everything

In 2021, I published a book called *No One Listens to Your Dad's Radio Show*. A classic fish-out-of-water story—an English DJ moves to Australia with his family, some funny stories about mid-life crises and how I went from no-one to number one.

I can tell that story in many ways. The polished version. The highlight reel. The version that makes me look good with punchlines.

Or I can tell you the truth.

The honest truth is funnier. More powerful. Has more wonder and connection.

It's also scary as shit.

Because to tell the real story, I had to talk about the panic attacks. How I couldn't do the radio show for a while. How, for a horrific time—a real dark night of the soul—it looked like I might have to actually stop doing live radio. After over 20 years. That's my joy. That's my happy place. That's my identity. Not doing that felt like not doing life.

I went and got help. I made my way back to myself and back on air. But I never shared that part of the story. I kept the truth hidden because I didn't want to feel judged, and really that means I didn't want to feel ashamed. But now something in me wanted to kill that shame script, the one with the funny jokes about men my age and midlife crisis. I stepped into my authenticity.

Guess what? Wasn't easy…

The warning

My wife Sarah tried to talk me out of it. For very valid reasons.

She said, 'You'll probably have panic attacks talking about this. You won't find it easy'.

She was right.

I did have panic attacks. And then I didn't. It became another layer of healing and transformation. But what I was really experiencing, underneath it all, was the residue of shame.

So I made a decision. I would lead with heart and vulnerability. The first three chapters of the book would be about the panic attacks. Front and centre. No hiding.

Product recall

Two days before the book came out, I saw a picture of myself in the Sunday newspaper profile about me and my book.

The headline: *Anxiety Silenced the DJ.*

I threw the newspaper on the floor. My face stung with shame.

Sarah saw it. Gave me that look. You know the one—the one that says, *Told you so.*

'Fuck,' I sighed. 'What have I done?'

She asked if I could get them to take the book off the shelves.

I said, 'Only if we break into every bookshop in Australia. And I don't think that's the point'.

There was a reason part of me had put that story in. I had to honour that, even if it scared me. Vulnerability is a calling. To deny it is our choice—and I have many times and will again—but we pay a price. We stay imprisoned. When we follow the call, our lives get better.

Crunchy and messy

The day the book came out, I tried to talk about it on the radio show.

It came out crunchy. So fucking messy. Tears.

This is what happens with real, spontaneous speaking—speaking from the heart. You find yourself surprised by what you're saying. You discover emotions you didn't know were fully there, or that you hadn't fully allowed.

That's what happened on that Tuesday morning. Live on air. No script. Just me, cracking open.

What people actually remember

Several years later, I'm still receiving emails about that book. Almost every day. And there's only one thing they talk about. Only one thing they connected to.

The vulnerability.

Not the life advice. Not the funny, well-crafted stories. Not the parenting wisdom. Not the number-one ratings victory.

The vulnerability. That's what moved them, that's what stayed with them.

That book changed my life. Changed the course of it. It's why you're reading this book in your hands right now. I was gifting something to my future self. And it all came through vulnerability and authenticity.

The ripple effect

The book got me onto podcasts, talking about vulnerability. About panic attacks. About asking for help. I loved it. Usually when I'm on those shows I'm in performance mode—I want to be a great guest and kill, as we say.

Sorry, the language of comedians is so dramatic. All 'killing', 'destroying', fear of 'bombing'. I guess me saying, 'I totally vulnerabled out there! *Just took the roof off and* authentically connected!' *doesn't have the same power.*

But now, there was something calling me to drop the script and allow presence over performance.

I went on *The Imperfects*—the biggest podcast in Australia for mental health. The boys were brilliant. They created a space where I could go deep.

And I left that interview with a vulnerability hangover. That familiar feeling: *You said too much. You were too vulnerable. You went too far. They're going to think you're weak.*

But without that podcast, there's no helping Rob the paramedic, who came to try to save my mother-in-law's life.

He'd listened to me on *The Imperfects*. Heard me talk about my panic attacks. It had helped him. Made him feel less odd, less alone. Changed his relationship with his own panic attacks.

The very story I regretted sharing had been exactly the story he needed to hear.

And then, a message from the host of another podcast:

> A friend wrote to me tonight to say he's left his house twice in the last few days to commit suicide. He's just listened to our podcast and it's made him rethink life. It's given him the 'courage' to carry on. I think your book and our conversation is helping a lot of men.

The story we don't want to share has such power to help others.

The crack I was so ashamed of became the light that reached someone in their darkest moment. Think back to what Dacher Keltner said (in chapter 7) about what moves us the most in wonder and awe—other people's stories of overcoming hardships.

The key

Vulnerability is a doorway. A doorway into deeper connection, deeper truth, deeper life.

But it's a door most of us keep locked. We installed the lock years ago—maybe in childhood, maybe after a heartbreak—and we've kept it locked ever since.

The key to that locked door? Courage.

Not confidence. Not certainty. Courage. The willingness to step through even though you're scared.

Vulnerability and courage are interwoven. You can't have one without the other. Courage isn't the absence of fear—it's the open-hearted willingness to move forward anyway. And vulnerability isn't weakness—it's the courage to be exactly who you are.

Sometimes, vulnerability asks you to loosen your grip. To let the ego fall away just enough to die a little. To go beyond your need to control others' perception of you. The old gatekeeper within you—anxiety, the one who once kept you safe by holding you back—now needs to hear the truth: your protection is no longer required.

The twins

Vulnerability has been a great guide and teacher for me. I had to work at that though. For a large part of my life my vulnerability was kept behind a boarded-up door with DO NOT ENTER in large letters.

Vulnerability shows up as twins: fear and truth.

When those two show up together, you know vulnerability is calling you forward. Deeper into your life. Deeper into your heart.

That's the signal. That's the invitation. Fear and truth, standing side by side, asking, *Will you come? Will you speak that scary truth you're holding onto?*

Two conditions. Both necessary.

First: it has to be *your* truth. Not what you think you should say. The actual thing that's true for you.

Second: it has to be *scary*. If it's not scary, it's not vulnerable—it's just information.

Vulnerability is the moment when fear and truth show up at the same time. And you act anyway.

My fear transformed into a source of quiet power. I discovered that people don't judge you nearly as harshly as you judge yourself.

When the book came out, I feared judgement. I braced for it. I was ready to be judged and feel ashamed.

And all I got was connection like I'd never felt before. I found gifts I didn't know I had.

I felt more seen than ever before. And I saw others like never before.

That's the thing nobody tells you about vulnerability. You think you're risking rejection. But what you're actually risking is being truly seen. And when people meet the real you—not the mask, not the performance, not the polished version—they don't run away. They lean in.

Allowing the fear

The first few times you practise being more vulnerable, it can be intense and scary. But a life with a closed heart isn't really a life at all. Your whole system may scream, *Don't do this.*

It will be a script trying to keep you safe. From judgement, from feeling shame.

The instinct is to slay the fear. Push through it. Conquer it.

Try this: fast-forward through your fear story. Play the whole horror movie. What actually happens if you say the truth? Usually, the catastrophe you imagine is far worse than anything real.

The shift comes from allowing fear. Feeling it fully. Being with it. Getting curious about it. Attuning to it the same way you'd attune to another person—with wonder, not warfare. Otherwise, we're at war with ourselves, and in that fight we always lose.

What does this fear actually feel like in my body? Where does it live? What is it trying to protect? How can I be with this from a place of kindness and self-compassion?

When you stop fighting the fear and start welcoming it, something remarkable happens. It transforms. Fear and excitement are almost identical in the body. The racing heart. The heightened senses. The only difference is the story we tell about it.

The story you're scared to tell

There's a story you're scared to tell.

I know there is. We all have one. Maybe more than one.

Most of the time we're stuck, it's because two stories are stuck. The old script of who we thought we were, and the new story of who we are becoming.

That story is your calling. It's asking you to shed it, the way a snake sheds old skin. Because that story is keeping you too small.

I know—because I had that story too. The panic attacks. The dark night. The fear that I might have to give up the thing I loved most.

Then there was another one—about being a superman leader, not showing vulnerability to my team or it would freak them out. I told them the story and how I would lead with heart and vulnerability instead. This made my connection with my team better right away.

The story that used to own me became the story I could share. And in sharing it, I gave others permission to share theirs.

Everything you love

Think about everything you love in your life.

Your partner. Your children. Your closest friendships. The work that lights you up. The dream you haven't told anyone about yet.

Every single one of them requires you to be vulnerable. Every show I start, every story I tell, every joke I make is an act of vulnerability.

To love your partner is to risk losing them. To love your children is to know they will grow and leave. To pursue work you care about is to risk rejection. To share your creative work is to hand someone a piece of your soul.

We are what we love, not what loves us.

And what we love can make us or break us. That's the deal. There's no version of deep love—of anything—that comes with a guarantee.

The most vulnerable act

When I became a dad, that's when vulnerability got really present.

You hold this tiny person and suddenly you understand: you have never been more exposed in your life. Your heart is now walking around outside your body. And there's nothing you can do to protect yourself from how much you love them.

The most vulnerable act is letting love in.

Not giving it. Letting it in.

Love requires openness. Openness requires courage. Courage requires vulnerability.

It's a circle. Each one leads to the next. You can't skip a step.

We think vulnerability is about what we express outwardly. But real vulnerability goes both ways. It's also about receiving. Letting someone see you and still want to be there. Letting compliments land instead of deflecting them. Letting help arrive instead of insisting you're fine.

Your connectability

Vulnerability is needed to live a life worth living. Not half-lived. Actually lived.

To start a new dream. A new adventure. A new conversation. A radio show on the other side of the world. A marriage. Parenthood.

To read a eulogy. To get up in front of teammates. To tell a friend you're struggling.

Vulnerability is your connectability.

It's your hand outreached. Sometimes to help unknown hands who needed your story, your truth. Hands you'll never shake. People you'll never meet. Lives you'll never know you touched.

I spent years rehearsing the perfect version of myself.

Turns out nobody wanted tickets to that show. They wanted the blooper reel.

The stories I was sure would make people run away? They're the ones that made people lean in.

Unfolders

Three questions to sit with:

1. Where are fear and truth showing up together in your life right now? That's vulnerability calling.
2. What's the old script you have about vulnerability?
3. What are you worried people would see if you let yourself be a little more vulnerable?

10

Enjoyment

The word 'enjoy' comes from the Old French *enjoir*, meaning 'to give joy to' or 'to take delight in'. It's made up of two parts: *en-*, meaning 'to put into', and *joir*, meaning 'to experience joy'.

So, 'enjoy' literally means to put yourself into joy. To put joy into something. To be it. Not to wait for joy to arrive. Not to earn it. Not to deserve it first.

To step into it. Actively. Now.

How much do you enjoy your life?

Big question, isn't it?

What nobody told you

Think about every piece of advice you've ever been given about speaking, presenting, communicating, connecting. What did it teach you?

Prepare. Practise. Plan what you're going to say. Control your nerves. Manage the room. Read your audience. Be professional. Be polished. Be appropriate. Get. It. Right.

Nobody—not once—said, 'Oh, remember to enjoy yourself'.

And that's the whole problem.

Because enjoyment is the signal that you've arrived. It's the moment you stop performing and start being present.

Enjoyment flips the whole table. It says, 'Connection comes alive when *you* come alive'.

The problem with getting good at managing

Here's a line that stopped me cold when I first heard it during the great business coach Joe Hudson's Art of Accomplishment course:

'The problem with getting good at managing your life is that you end up with a life that has to be managed.'

I spent years managing. Managing my career. Managing my image. Managing conversations.

Exhausting.

Some years ago, I went to Blue Derby in Tasmania with my mate Adam. One-hundred kilometres of world-class mountain-bike trails through rainforests for three days. We were going for the riding, stunning nature and beers in the evening around a fire. We had no idea that we would be doing hours of intense and beautiful biking on the equivalent of a ski-slopes black run.

I also didn't expect life lessons in the mud.

Early on, the instructors told me to stop being so rigid on the bike or I'd be fighting it, making everything harder. Enjoy the ride—stop being so controlling, it's more dangerous. I was scared. We were speeding through world-class courses and I had no idea how to handle the speeding chaos of rocks, tree stumps, sudden 30-foot drops down sheer cliff faces. On the first day, me and my mate, the oldest in the group by a decade or more, were held back to work on our 'core skills'.

We felt like the kids who had to repeat the year. A child instructor taught us how to brake. Our egos!

I was getting philosophy lessons from muddy 19- and 21-year-old guides. I loved every second.

The lesson that stuck? I kept stumbling in the early runs, slamming on brakes to avoid rocks and stumps. Bike buddha Finn whispered, 'Stop looking down. Look where you want to go and trust that your body knows how to get you there. Flowing all the way, soft grip, enjoy the ride'.

Stop looking down. Stop steering so hard. Trust that you know how to get there.

On the last day, all eight of us were cycling through an icy Tasmanian river along a very thin ledge.

'Momentum is the focus here,' was the yelled instruction.

I tensed up as my wheel got close to the guy in front of me.

And suddenly, while I sat on my mountain bike, I toppled over sideways into a fucking ice-cold Tasmanian river. Still sitting on the bike. Fully submerged.

All I could hear was laughter.

As I freed myself from the titanic wreckage of the mountain bike, Finn helped me out. A 21-year-old boy rescuing a middle-aged man, soaking wet, shivering, ego dripping.

He just looked at me and said, 'Your body is smarter than you'.

'That isn't hard,' I gurgled.

Then he asked, 'Do you grip your radio show as tight as you grip this bike?'

I said, 'No'.

He said, 'Then ungrip. Enjoy the ride, it's easier and safer'.

Pretty good, hey?

Mountain biking guru. If that's a thing, Finn was it.

The Four Es

Several years ago, I found myself trying to devise a framework to reconnect with my radio show.

If you're fortunate enough to find work that brings you joy and meaning, your relationship with it is like any other relationship. It undergoes seasons—summers of flourishing, springs of growth, autumns of transition and winters of barrenness.

I was in the winter phase.

To reignite the warmth, I did what I always do when I'm lost: I quieted down and listened.

One day, I started to sketch a compass with four Es.

- *Energise.* That came easily. Breakfast radio is about energy—energise the audience, energise myself, energise my words. Good intention. It made sense.
- *Exaggerate.* I love telling stories; I've spent my life doing it. Years ago, some professor of storytelling told me that people expect exaggeration in stories—they enjoy it more knowing it's exaggerated. That's been my life. It drives my wife and family nuts when they hear me tell a story on air that's not quite what happened. 'He's exaggerated that,' they say. And I'm like, 'Yeah, that's the job. I'm a professional exaggerator'. So, if my daughter's room is a bit messy, on air it's a squalid pit where even rats wouldn't go. If my wife is powerful in our relationship, she's more powerful than Darth Vader—Darth Vader would fear her.
- *Entertain.* You might think, how bad was your radio show that you needed reminding to entertain? But sometimes you do need reminding. Making five shows a week, three hours a day, it can become routine. Reminding yourself to entertain adds attention to my stories and hosting.

Energise. Exaggerate. Entertain.

Then I wrote down a fourth word: *Enjoy.*

And something interesting happened.

I stared at that word and my inner critic, you know, that lovely voice in your head, said *that's wrong*...

Some bullying manager part of me didn't think I was entitled to enjoy my own radio show. As if suffering meant working hard enough. As if exhaustion was proof of value.

The guilt we inherit

Many of us feel guilty when things feel good.

If you grew up around struggle or sacrifice, joy can feel... wrong. Like you're breaking some unspoken rule.

I saw my mum and dad work so hard. A lot of their working life was endurance. My mum as an NHS nurse doing back-breaking work. My dad worked in a car factory before automation—two weeks of day shift, two weeks of night shift, working his backside off. For years before we had a car, he would cycle to work. A two-hour round trip. Then a 12-hour shift.

I felt guilty enjoying my work.

That belief nearly broke me many, many times. I mistook grinding for virtue. Burnout a consequence from hard work done well.

Along with our scripts, both known and unknown, we have these vows we unwittingly take on and agree to. We can renegotiate and break them at any time.

The vow

On the long flight emigrating to Australia—one-way ticket, London to Melbourne—I had time to reflect on my 20 years of UK radio and how I hadn't allowed myself to enjoy it lately. Too often chasing the next big idea, ratings, awards, endless drive for better content.

Much of those 20 years had been about building something. A career. Providing for my family. Proving myself. All good things. But somewhere along the way, I'd stopped enjoying it. I was surviving my dream job instead of living it.

Somewhere over the ocean, I made a new vow. Gave away old ones no longer serving me.

I would tear up the script that said I needed to work very hard and be exhausted or else I was doing it wrong. I would give myself permission to enjoy this wild ride, regardless of the outcome.

Enjoyment became not just a point on my compass. It became my North Star.

Years earlier, someone had already told me this. But I wasn't ready to hear it at the time.

In the early 2000s, early in my career, I had just got a London breakfast show on the only station I wanted to work on, XFM. In my six incredible years there I met Ricky Gervais and Stephen Merchant—they did a weekend show with my team member Karl Pilkington. They went on to make the world's biggest podcast. Also on XFM was the guy doing the evening show who now runs Apple Music, Zane Lowe.

One day I got a phone call that changed my life. Someone said one of my radio and TV heroes wanted to meet me. A few hours later I'm in this legend's house and we get chatting. He offers me a TV show on the spot. I'd never been on TV in my life. Live, five nights a week. I said yes.

But that's not what changed my life.

We got chatting—and you have to understand the enormity at the time of just being in front of this guy; to this day I still see him as one of the greatest TV and radio hosts of all time. Chris Evans—and he said he'd been listening to my radio show. He complimented me on how funny it was; then he said something that was the game changer:

Are you enjoying it though? It's funny, but to me I hear a guy not letting himself enjoy it.

Sometimes in a conversation someone says something so piercingly true it goes right through any emotional armour you're wearing and right to your heart. It changes you. It may take you some time to put yourself back together. Those words did.

Years later, I read a book on another hero of mine, Dave Letterman—how he regrets now he never enjoyed his chat show more.

Play fucking loud

Around that time, I read about Bob Dylan going electric. You know the story—he plugged in at the Newport Folk Festival and the folk purists lost their minds. Heckling. Booing. Betrayal.

During a show in Manchester, the crowd was relentless. Someone yelled, 'Judas!' Dylan turned to his band and said four words: 'Play it fucking loud'.

That's Bob saying enjoy it even more. When they're throwing things at you, when nothing's going your way, when the crowd wants you to be someone you're not—lean in. Turn it up. Enjoy the hell out of it.

That became my mantra in those early Australian months.

Play it fucking loud.

During a show I would write PFL for short on a sticky note. My polite way to rebel.

Enjoyment is *how*, not *what*

The world teaches us, 'Do what you enjoy'. Find your passion. Follow your bliss.

That's not wrong, exactly. But it's incomplete.

Because here's the flip:

Enjoying is not about what *you're doing. It's about* how *you're doing it.*

You can enjoy taking out the bins. You can enjoy paying a bill. You can enjoy a difficult conversation. You can enjoy being wrong. You can do what I do when I screw up live on air, or the show's wheels are coming off—enjoy it. It's humanising. It's funny.

Or you can hate all of those things.

The activity doesn't determine the enjoyment. Your presence does.

I've had incredible guests on my show—famous, fascinating people—and felt nothing. Going through the motions. And I've had random Tuesday morning calls with listeners who lit me up from the inside. Same job. Same microphone. Completely different experience.

The difference wasn't what I was doing. It was whether I was enjoying it.

Enjoyment is contagious

People want to be around people who are enjoying themselves. Match this with vulnerability, attunement and wonder, and you have something magnetic.

Not performing enjoyment. Not pretending to have fun. Actually enjoying the moment you're in. Just even a little more.

People relax around someone who's enjoying themselves. People trust someone who's enjoying themselves. People follow someone who's enjoying themselves.

Your enjoyment is the anchor frequency everyone else calibrates to.

It's leadership without force. Connection without effort.

The conversation about joy

Last year I had a tough conversation with an awesome team member. They were in the wrong role but convinced they were right for it—a job title they thought they'd always wanted, but one that was making them stressed, and the team wasn't functioning well.

Without a script, we talked about team structure and their zones of genius—the parts they actually loved. And then I asked a simple question: 'Are you enjoying this? Because it seems like it's killing you'.

Tears came.

And then we started having an honest conversation. A proper one. Not about job titles or career ladders. About finding joy again. We created a new way for them to get back to their genius. They have been in full flow ever since.

That's what enjoyment does. It cuts through the bullshit. It gets you to the truth faster than any management technique ever could.

Stop managing. Start enjoying.

When you enjoy the conversation, the conversation enjoys you back.

When you enjoy the person, they open up.

When you enjoy the moment, the moment expands.

When you enjoy yourself, everything becomes possible.

Unfolders

Three questions to sit with:

1. Where in your life are you managing when you could be enjoying more?
2. What vows or scripts do you think you have about how hard you have to work in your life?
3. What's one conversation this week you could enter into with the sole intention of enjoying it?

11

Surf

Like the ocean, a conversation is a living, breathing, organic movement.

Wild, tidal, powerful. Unpredictable. Irrational. Emotional. Volatile. Sometimes chaotic. It's all of life.

One moment you're gliding, the next moment everything's changed—the energy, the tone, the direction. A word lands wrong. An emotion surfaces. Someone goes quiet. Someone goes loud.

You can't plan for what's coming. You can only respond to what's emerging here right now.

That's *surfing.*

I love watching documentaries about surfing. Since moving to Australia, I see surfers way more often than when I lived in the UK.

In one documentary, a several-time world champion—tanned, muscular, basically a Greek god—looked into the camera and told me, a fellow Greek god eating corn chips on my couch, something I've never forgotten: you don't need confidence to surf. You need trust.

I see confidence as 'I know I can do this'. It's certainty. It's feeling prepared.

Trust is more 'I don't know how this will go, but I'll be all right'. It's faith. It's feeling grounded.

Confidence comes from the past—from having done it before. You've done the reps.

Trust comes from the present—from being here now.

Surfers don't wait to feel confident before they paddle out. They trust the wave will teach them. They trust themselves to respond wisely.

That's what WAVES asks of you.

Tree, true, trust

I was curious about the word 'trust'. Where it comes from. What it actually means.

Turns out, it comes from Old Norse—*traust*—meaning confidence, help, protection.

But here's what lit me up: *trust shares the same ancient root as 'tree' and 'true'.*

All three words come from the same place. An Indo-European root meaning 'firm, solid, steadfast'.

Like wood. Like a tree. Like something rooted in the ground.

Trust = to be firm, solid, reliable.

Tree = something solid and rooted.

True = firm, steadfast, not false.

They're all the same thing. All about being grounded. Rooted. Real.

Then I looked up 'faith'. The original root meant 'to trust, to confide, to persuade'.

A verb. Not a noun.

Not 'I have faith' but 'I am faithing'—actively trusting, actively moving forward, actively placing confidence in something before you have proof.

Faith as action. Not possession.

You don't wait to have trust and then start. You start, and through the starting—through the faithing—you learn you can do it.

That's surfing. That's speaking. You commit to the wave before you know if you'll make it.

The playground

Watch children talk to each other.

No scripts. No agenda. No 'let me prepare my key points before I approach this sandbox'.

They just... play. They respond to what's happening. They say what they feel. They change direction mid-sentence because something more interesting showed up. They laugh. They fight. They make up. They're fully there.

Children are natural surfers. Natural faithers.

Then something happens. School. Jobs. 'Professionalism'. We learn that conversations have stakes. That words have consequences. That we need to manage how we come across. There is right and wrong. Wrong makes you feel stupid or shame. So, try and avoid that.

So, we start scripting. Planning. Rehearsing. Protecting.

And somewhere along the way, we forget how to play.

WAVES isn't learning something new. It's remembering something old. The part of you that knew how to be present before anyone told you presence was a skill.

The surfer was already in you. You just buried them under years of scripts.

The biggest shift I've made in my entire career is from performance to presence.

For years I was a performer. Witty. Fast. Sharp. Always preparing. Always anticipating. Always ready with the next bit, the next line, the next joke. Performance kept me safe. Performance kept me impressive. Performance kept me in control.

But I wasn't surfing anything. I was stage-managing the ocean. It was exhausting and regularly led to burnout.

Surfers can only ride waves by being present. They cannot steer the ocean. They cannot control what's coming. They can only be there—fully, completely—meeting the moment.

Same with connection. Same with conversation.

You cannot control another person. You cannot make a conversation go where you want it to go. You can only be present to what's actually happening. And respond from there.

Because real connection only happens in the unscripted now.

Scripts make you stiff. WAVES makes you limber.

You will wipe out

We overthink and overprepare our speaking because otherwise it could go wrong. You don't want to stumble or lose your way.

I've been speaking for a living for decades and I get it 'wrong' and fall off every day. Doesn't matter. They don't want me to be perfect, they want to connect to me.

You will fall off.

You'll lose your words mid-sentence. You'll say the wrong thing. You'll misread the wave completely. You'll go left when you should have gone right. You'll commit to a wave that closes out on you.

This isn't failure.

This is life.

Watch a seasoned surfer. If they fall off, they don't head for the shore and go home. They just carry on.

Every surfer wipes out. Every single one. The ones who get good are the ones who paddle back out.

I watched Roger Federer being interviewed once and he said his greatest strength was his recovery shots. Not his serve. Not his forehand. His ability to recover when things went wrong.

I wipe out on live radio. Regularly. In front of hundreds of thousands of people. I lose my train of thought. I say something clumsy. I miss the moment entirely. Either I don't mention it and carry on, pausing, resetting, summarising. Or I laugh at what just happened—I use that mistake as a chance to connect.

The magic is in the mess.

And then I paddle back out.

Because that's the job. That's the practice. That's life.

Wipeouts aren't the opposite of surfing. They're part of surfing.

Love over will

Here's the thing that took me years to understand:

You cannot build trust by waiting to feel it.

You build trust by acting as if you have it. By faithing before you're ready. By committing to the wave even though you might fall.

Every time you do that—every time you start without waiting to feel confident—you prove to yourself: I can do this. The words come. I survive. I thrive.

In an interview with Howard Stern, Jerry Seinfeld was asked if he willed his way to success.

> What you were using, what Michael Jordan uses and what I use, is not will. It's love. When you love something, it's a bottomless pool of energy … Will is like not eating dessert … Love is endless. Will is finite.

That's it. That's the whole secret.

You can't will your way to authentic connection. You can't technique your way there. You can only love your way there.

That's what WAVES becomes when you stop treating it like a checklist and start letting it live in you.

Wonder. Attunement. Vulnerability. Enjoyment. Surf.

Not steps. States.

When you've practised WAVES enough, something shifts. You stop thinking about it.

Wonder becomes how you see.

Attunement becomes how you listen.

Vulnerability becomes how you show up.

Enjoyment becomes how you hold yourself.

And Surf? Surfing becomes instinct. Intuition. Wisdom in real time.

You feel the conversation turning and you turn with it. You sense the wave building and you're already paddling. You don't know how you knew—you just knew.

That's not technique. That's embodiment.

That's insight in action.

This becomes embodied. It's not about what you do. It's about how you want to be.

That's my life.

Every morning, I paddle out. I don't know what's coming. Some days the waves are huge—big guests, breaking news, calls that crack open into something real. Some days it's flat. Some days I wipe out spectacularly.

But I keep paddling out.

Because the ocean is always there. The waves keep coming. And the ride—when you catch it—is the best feeling in the world.

The ride

The best conversations don't happen because you perform well or control the moment.

They happen because you showed up. Present. Open. Alive.

Because you wondered instead of assumed.

Because you attuned instead of projected.

Because you got vulnerable instead of defended.

Because you enjoyed yourself instead of managing yourself and others.

Because you surfed instead of scripted.

That's WAVES.

That's connection.

You don't need to wait to feel trust. You faith your way forward.

Your next great conversation is waiting. Paddle out.

Unfolders

Three questions to sit with:

1. What are you waiting to feel ready for?
2. Where have you forgotten how to play?
3. Who's waiting to meet the real you?

PART III
Transmission and reception

12

Worse than death

There's that old classic Jerry Seinfeld joke about how public speaking is the number one fear, ahead of death. Which means at a funeral, most people would rather be in the coffin than giving the eulogy.

It's funny because it's absurd. And it's funny because ... somewhere in us, we get it.

Why? What is it about standing up and speaking that feels worse than death itself?

I asked my listeners and followers what were their biggest anxieties about speaking. Thousands of responses came in. And they all came down to one thing.

Fear.

Not four different fears. Not a dozen varieties. One fear, wearing different masks. The fear of being seen. The fear of being judged. The fear of being found out.

If you want to understand why speaking feels terrifying for so many of us, you have to go deeper than technique. Deeper than communication tips. Deeper than performance psychology.

You have to go to the story behind the fear. To the source of it all.

The belonging fear

Almost every speaking fear is a belonging fear in disguise.

Thousands of years ago, if you said the wrong thing in front of the tribe—'Anyone else here thinking about going vegan?'—you were out. And out meant dead.

In a tribe of 80 to 150 people, loss of status meant loss of protection. Loss of protection meant danger. Danger meant death.

It really was a matter of life and death.

Your nervous system remembers this.

It doesn't care that you're standing on a stage and the audience are accountants from Adelaide, not warriors from 12 000 BCE. Whether you're doing a best man's speech, taking the team meeting, asking a question on a Teams call. It reacts as if your life depends on this moment.

Which is why modern speaking fears feel disproportionately huge. Your body thinks the stakes are survival. Your brain thinks the answer is perfection. And in that gap—between biology and belief—fear grows.

Where it lives

Here's something important. All of this fear—the anxiety, the nerves, the dread—it's not in your head. It's in your body.

Feel it now if you can. Think about something that makes you nervous. A conversation you've been avoiding. A presentation coming up. Speaking up in a meeting.

Where do you feel it?

For most of us, it lives in the centre line. From your belly button up into the middle of your chest. That's where the static broadcasts from. The tightness. The constriction. The butterflies. The adrenaline surge looking for somewhere to go.

Most of us try to think our way out of this. We try to logic the fear away. *It'll be fine. What's the worst that can happen? You've done this before.*

Doesn't work, does it?

Because you can't use logic on an emotional issue. Fear isn't a thinking problem. It's a feeling problem. Or more accurately—it's a feeling invitation. To allow the fear, to fully feel it and let it move, to receive help and compassion from yourself.

And the way out is down, not up. Out of the head, into the body.

Sometimes it's as simple as putting a hand on your solar plexus—or in the middle of your chest, around your heart—and just naming what you feel.

I have adrenaline.

I'm scared, and that's okay.

Researchers at UCLA found that when people put their feelings into words—simply naming 'I'm angry' or 'I'm scared'—their amygdala, the brain's alarm system, calmed down. The act of labelling the emotion activated the prefrontal cortex, which helps regulate emotional responses. It's like your body goes, *Oh, you noticed. You're paying attention. Okay. We can work with this.*

You're not trying to fix it. You're not trying to make it go away. You're just acknowledging it. Meeting it with compassion, like you would if your child or friend came to you saying they were nervous.

The worthiness wound

But here's what's really underneath all of it.

The fear isn't really about messing up. It's about what messing up would mean.

If I stumble, they'll think I'm incompetent.

If I forget my words, they'll see I'm a fraud.

If I'm not impressive, they won't respect me.

If it goes wrong… I'll be unlovable. Exiled. Ashamed. Humiliated.

Do you see it?

Every speaking fear is really a worthiness fear. A safety fear. The static that says who you are isn't enough. And that means… exile.

And that's the real wound. Not the nerves. Not the sweaty palms. The belief—somewhere deep down—that if people saw the real you, the unscripted you, the you without the polish and the preparation… they wouldn't like you.

So we reach for scripts. No wonder—of course we would. We over-prepare. We try to become someone else when we speak. Someone more impressive. More polished. More… acceptable.

But here's what I've learned, and it took me decades and a breakdown to learn it:

Even if it went wrong, you would be okay.

The teacher

I know exactly where my wound started.

I was 10 years old, standing at the front of the class, reading my book report out loud. I'd worked hard on it. I was nervous but proud.

When I finished, the teacher—let's call her Mrs Catshit Breath (my editor insisted I change her name for legal reasons)—looked at me and said, 'I think you can do better than that'.

That was it. No feedback. No kindness. Just dismissal.

I walked back to my seat with my face burning red, trying to suck the tears back in through my eyes, and down somewhere those feelings got buried.

That little fella is still in me.

Any time my ratings go down, you know who struggles with that more than the grown-up me who's experienced the ups and downs so many times? Him. Part of me is still stuck up there, right after Mrs Catshit Breath dismissed me so casually. Holding my breath. Frozen.

That's the thing about these wounds — they don't stay in the past. They live in us. And every time we stand up to speak, that 10-year-old is watching, waiting to see if it's safe this time.

The good news? He doesn't need you to protect him anymore. He needs you to show him it turned out okay. That you survived. That you even learned to love it.

That's the healing. Not fixing the fear — but letting that younger version of you see who you've become.

Most of us, when we speak, are in Impress Mode. This causes so much constriction in your body. Being fixated on a particular outcome. Presenting a version of yourself to impress the others that you're professional, smart, confident.

Impress Mode asks, *How do I look? What do they think of me? Am I getting this right?*

And it's exhausting. Because you're trying to manage something you can't control — other people's perceptions. Good luck with that! You're performing instead of connecting. You're so busy monitoring how it's landing that you're not actually here.

Communication is about expression. Your life should be you expressing the fullness of you, because that's what brings us alive.

The alternative is Express Mode.

Focused on how you want to feel. Let that be your goal. On what wants to come through you. On being present to the moment and what you're excited to be sharing. On serving rather than proving.

Express Mode asks, *How do I want to feel right now? What wants to be expressed? How can I be here, fully, with these people?*

Impress Mode creates static. Express Mode clears it.

The shift isn't about being confident. It's about being present. It's about getting out of your head—where all the worry about perception lives—and dropping into the moment. Into your body. Into what's actually happening. Getting in contact with what's seeking expression from you.

This old story really helped me

There's an old story about a Tibetan yogi named Milarepa that's helped me so much, and I've passed it on to many people.

Milarepa had been meditating in caves. One day, he left his cave to gather firewood. When he came back, his cave had been overtaken by demons. Demons everywhere. Don't you hate it when that happens?

His first thought: *I have to get rid of these demons. I've got the guys coming over later and it's going to be weird.*

So he starts lunging at them, chasing them, trying to slay them, to drive them out. But the demons don't give a fuck. They are completely unfazed. In fact, the more he chases them, the more comfortable and settled they seem to become.

Realising that fighting isn't working, Milarepa tries a different approach. He decides to teach them a lesson. If chasing them out won't work, maybe hearing the teachings will change their minds.

So he sits down and begins teaching them about existence, non-existence, non-duality, compassion, kindness, the nature of impermanence...

The demons just stare at him with their huge, bulging eyes. Not one of them is leaving.

At this point, Milarepa lets out a deep breath of surrender. He realises he can't manipulate these demons into leaving. Maybe he has something to learn from them.

He looks deeply into the eyes of each demon, bows and says, 'Looks like we're going to be here together. I surrender to whatever it is you're here for me to learn'.

In that moment, all but one of the demons disappears.

The biggest, scariest, fiercest demon remains. This one's got big, bulging eyes, flaring nostrils and huge dripping fangs. He ain't going nowhere.

Milarepa's starting to understand something now. He surrenders even more.

He walks over to the largest demon. He looks into its terrible face. And then—holding nothing back—he places his head right into the demon's mouth.

Eat me if you wish.

And at that moment, the demon bows and disappears.

Eat me

I think about Milarepa a lot when I'm feeling nervous.

Because that's what we try to do with our fear, isn't it? First we fight it. We try to slay it, push through it, power past it. Chase it away. *Just be confident. Don't be nervous. Get over it.*

Doesn't work for everyone. Not me.

Then we try to outsmart it. We prepare more. We rehearse more. We create scripts and back-up plans and techniques. *If I just have enough material, the fear won't get me.*

Doesn't work either.

The demons don't care about your preparation. They're not impressed by your techniques.

The only thing that works is surrender. Walking toward the fear. Looking it in the eyes. Saying, *Eat me if you wish.*

Not fighting it. Not fixing it. Not fleeing from it.

Facing it. Something dissolves a little when you do.

The Upfronts

People are stunned when I say even after so long in live broadcasting, sometimes I still get nervous. Let me tell you about a few weeks ago.

I found myself backstage in a vast room, surrounded by very important people. Money people. Important to my job, my career and judging from the nerves coming from my bosses, important to God. The atmosphere was buzzing with energy, yet I felt utterly isolated. Unable to speak to anyone. I went very quiet. It was as if I had retreated back into that cave, surrounded by all those demons. Despite trying all my techniques, one of those bloody demons still lingered beside me backstage, invisible to everyone else.

Let me take you there.

The big TV networks in the United States have an annual event called the Upfronts, where they present next year's shows to advertisers and clients. Media journalists. It's a huge deal. Our new CEO, a man who likes to be called Stevo (in Australia, adding an O at the end of someone's name is common—don't ask me why) had invested heavily in these Upfronts. Months of preparation. They were presenting to 1200 people in a big theatre in Sydney—the first-ever radio network in the world to do Upfronts.

I wanted to impress these people. Sydney is the city where my breakfast show would air next year. A tough and cynical room.

I had three minutes on stage and there were around 10 different speakers from the company, all using autocue.

They were stunned when I said I didn't want any autocue.

They asked why.

I explained that I'm writing a book called *Unscript* about authentic, spontaneous speaking. Using an autocue would contradict my book's message.

So when I walked out there, the autocue simply read *Christian O'Connell speaks*. And then it was blank.

The stakes were high and so was the expectation. All day long, people patted me on my back saying how excited they were to see what I'd do because of my stand-up comedy background.

Then—literally a minute before going on stage, in this massive theatre with cameras everywhere and a big megascreen behind me—someone very senior put a hand on my shoulder and said, 'This has to go well'.

Fuck me.

The demon with the fangs, right there. One minute before I walk out. Thanks for that.

And at that moment, I thought of Milarepa.

Eat me!

It made me smile.

Quietly, to myself, backstage, surrounded by all those important people and that one lingering demon, I said it: *Eat me!*

I forgot I was mic'd up so the whole tech crew heard and looked at me, a little concerned. I smiled back acknowledging I'd made it a little weird.

The smile was the shift. Something released. The static cleared, just a little.

And then I added something else, silently, to the person who'd just put their hand on my shoulder:

Fuck you.

Not anger. Just… fire. Defiance. And connecting to what I wanted to share out there. From my heart.

And I walked out onto that stage.

How did it go?

I died on my backside, got fired, my wife left me, my kids said they don't want to see me again. I now host a nightly pub quiz and meat raffle in a biker's bar.

No, here's what happened.

I walked out to give a talk on authentic connection. And the first thing I did was ... authentically connect.

I looked at the room. Twelve-hundred people. A casino. Four in the afternoon. And I said, 'So, this is where you come for a heartfelt talk on authentic connection. To a casino. At 4 in the afternoon. A place where dreams die. Much like radio'.

The room exploded.

And in that moment, all the demons gave me a chef's kiss each.

Why humour works

Humour does something almost magical to a room, and to us. When people laugh together, their nervous systems relax. Simultaneously. It's like a collective exhale. The barriers come down. The defences soften. Suddenly everyone's on the same side.

That's why humour is such a powerful antidote to the worthiness wound. Because the laughter is proof. Proof that you belong. Proof that the tribe isn't going to exile you.

Your nervous system gets the message: *We're safe here. These are our people.*

The 50 000-year-old fear loosens its grip.

And suddenly you can breathe. And speak. And be yourself.

And here's what's beautiful: being funny is actually a brave act. It takes courage. On that word, people misunderstand it.

The word 'courage' comes from the Latin *cor*—heart. Courage literally means 'full heart'. Not fearlessness. Fullness. Having your whole heart in it. How full is your heart?

That's the choice. Not confidence over fear. Full heart over empty performance.

Standing backstage, the demon breathing down my neck, I reconnected to my heart. I realised that unscripted is braver than autocue. That I'd rather fail being myself than succeed being someone else.

That rekindled my fire. That fire filled my heart. And from that full heart, I chose action.

I remembered 24 years ago first coming to Sydney, dreaming about doing a radio show here. Twenty-four years later I'm walking out onto a stage to announce I'm doing just that. I smiled to myself, at the path taken. Gratitude filled my heart. I spoke from that and began…

The Archer

Part of the fear of speaking is the very real concern about forgetting your words, or drying up.

I've learned to prepare for any talk—online, in person, on stage—using what I simply call The Archer.

Ten years ago, I read a book called *The Rise*, by Sarah Lewis. It's about mastery—what it actually takes to get great at something. She opens the book at a Columbia University archery practice, watching archers shoot for hours, aiming for that tiny 10 ring that looks like a matchstick from a distance.

And I found myself underlining half the book because everything she said about great archers… I'd discovered the hard way about speaking.

Here's what struck me most.

The best archers have what's called 'split vision'. They're holding two things at once—the target they're aiming for *and* the likely arc of the arrow's flight. They're not just staring at the bullseye. They're feeling the whole journey the arrow will take to get there. Utter presence.

When you over-memorise a speech—stare too hard at your notes, your script, the exact words you've planned to say—you lose the arc. You lose the flight. You lose the feel of where this is actually going to land with these particular people in this particular room.

But here's the bit that really got me.

Lewis talks about something called 'gold fever'. Also known as 'target panic'. It's what happens when an archer gets good—really good—and starts wanting gold so badly that they freeze. They choke. One day they're hitting tens, the next day they can't shoot at all. The wanting gets in the way of the doing.

Sound familiar?

That's what happened backstage at the Upfronts. I had my target. I had my arrows. I was ready. And then someone put their hand on my shoulder and said, 'This really needs to go well'—and suddenly I wanted it too much. Gold fever. Target panic. I became outcome dependent, rather than focused on how I wanted to feel.

Lewis puts it perfectly: 'Success is hitting that 10 ring. But mastery is knowing it means nothing if you can't hit it again and again'.

Mastery isn't about one perfect shot. It's about the practice. The process. The constant pursuit.

So here's how The Archer works. It's a way to get ready without gripping so tight that you get gold fever. A way to aim without losing the arc.

Three steps.

Step 1: Identify the target

What needs to land? If they remember only *one* thing, what should it be?

I ask myself: What shift in thinking, feeling or action do I want to create? Not just information transfer—transformation.

For the Upfronts, my target was simple: to show that my radio show is about authentic connection and shared experience, and then to show how my show amplifies that through Connection, Comedy and Conversation. Three Cs, three arrows.

If you don't know what your talk is about, or it's trying to do several things, that's putting static in your signal. Crystal clarity of target determines everything.

Step 2: Sharpen your arrows

Stories are your ammunition. That's how we connect best—not with more data or by over-explaining. But they need a point—literally, where does this story pierce the target? Sharper the arrows, easier their flight and impact.

For each arrow I ask: Does this support the bullseye? Is this a story or a set of information? What's my relationship to this story?

I had my arrows ready. Not scripted word for word, but sharp. I knew the moments I wanted to hit. The feelings I wanted to land.

Step 3: Prepare The Archer

Now here's the thing.

Target and arrows—that's the prep most people do. I'm not the first to look at archery and make a comparison to life and even to speaking, but most people miss something. The arrows and targets matter, but something matters more. Know your main point, line up your supporting stories. It's good advice. It's necessary.

But it's not enough.

Because you can have the clearest target and the sharpest arrows and still miss. You can be perfectly prepared and still bomb. You can know exactly what you want to say and find the words won't come.

What's missing is The Archer.

This is the step most people skip. And it's the one that matters most.

Here's what archers know that speakers forget: your emotional state travels through everything you do.

You are the medium and the message. You are both The Archer and the arrows.

An anxious archer doesn't just feel nervous—they shoot nervously. Tension will live in the grip, breath, release. The arrow carries it all the way to the target. You can't hide it. You can't fake it. The arrow knows.

You are both bow and archer. Medium and message. There's no separating who you're being from what you're saying.

Your state is *your content.* So put your state over script.

So I ask myself, *What do I need to show up full? How can I get out of my head and into my heart, and speak from there?*

For the Upfronts, I knew I wanted to connect with humour first—that's how I open my heart and theirs. So I asked myself: what's absurd about this situation? What's funny that nobody's saying? I didn't script a joke. I just looked for the real.

A casino. 4 pm. A place where dreams die. Trying to talk about authentic connection.

The material was right there. I just had to be in the right state to see it.

The Archer's truth

Here's what I learned that day, standing in front of 1200 people with nothing but a target and my arrows and a nervous system that had almost betrayed me:

The preparation matters. Know your target. Sharpen your stories. Do what you need to show up full. Find your conviction.

But in the end, The Archer has to release.

You have to trust the arc. Trust that the arrow will go where it's going to go. Trust that all your preparation lives in you now—not in your notes, not in your script—in your heart.

You are the bow. Your state is the string. Your stories are the arrows.

And when you release from presence instead of performance—when you let go instead of grip—something happens that you couldn't have planned.

The arrow finds its target.

Not because you controlled every variable, but because you trusted the shot.

You can download my Archer Preparation Worksheet PDF for talks/presentations at www.christianoconnell.com/unscript. It's a fillable template for your target, arrows and archer prep.

Your public speaking toolkit

Here's what helps me when I'm doing a keynote or any kind of public speech. Some of these tips might help you too.

- *Name it.* Out loud if you can, silently if you can't. Put your hand gently on the centre of your chest. Read your state, then you can reset. *I have adrenaline. I'm scared. My chest is tight.* Naming it reassures your nervous system. This is about *allowing*—because it's your resistance to emotions that creates the pain.
- *The double breath.* This is favoured by me or, more impressively, Professor Andrew Huberman. Close your mouth. Take in two rapid back-to-back breaths—one huge one, then another little cheeky one on top. Then sigh out through your mouth. Like

opening a trap door. Letting a handbrake off. Do it five to seven times. It's a real quick release.

- *Feel your feet.* Literally. Physical grounding triggers emotional grounding. Feel the floor beneath you. Holding you. Sometimes I say to myself 'Where are my feet?' I put my attention into them. Wiggle your toes. Feel your connection to the ground. So much energy is up in your head. Shifting your attention helps.
- *Talk to someone.* If you're getting edgy backstage or before a meeting, talk to the people around you. It shifts your focus from your internal state. We get nervous system regulation — social calming — from connecting with others.
- *Focus on service.* This one phrase has saved me more times than I can count. One breath, and I'm back in flow. *It's not about me. It's about them. What can I give? How can I help?*
- *My heart will know what to do.* Sometimes I just hand it over. To my heart, to something higher, to whatever name works for me. I stop trying to figure it out with my head. I trust that something deeper knows.
- *Connect to the fire.* What do you actually want to say? What are you excited about sharing? Connect to the heat of your conviction. Let that warmth spread through you.
- *Imagine light meeting light.* I imagine there's a light in my heart, and I'm sharing it with all the other lights in everybody I'm speaking to. Hearts to hearts. I stop demonising the audience — they're not out to get me. They're on my side.

And if all else fails:

Eat me.

Walk towards the demon. Put your head in its mouth. Surrender to whatever it's here to teach you. And watch it bow and disappear.

Unfolders

Three questions to sit with, not to answer immediately:

1. What is the demon you're frightened to go up to and face? Not the surface fear—the deeper one. What do you believe it would mean about you if things went wrong?
2. Think of a time you said 'eat me' without knowing it—when you stopped fighting the fear and just...went anyway. What shifted? What opened up?
3. If you truly believed that who you are is enough—that even if it went wrong, you'd be okay—how would you show up differently?

13

The heart of listening

Listening is the single most unappreciated and undervalued quality of connection.

My performance got dramatically better when I realised the importance of listening. For me, it's an anchor into presence.

How you listen determines how well you connect.

In my job, there is so much emphasis on the speaking part, but nothing about how we are going to listen.

What's true in live radio is also true in so many areas of life. When we go into a meeting, or a chat with a team member, partner or child, we over-index thinking about what we're going to say. We work on the presentation. We rehearse our points. We prepare our arguments.

But we spend almost no time thinking about how we listen.

Which is strange, when you think about it. Because how we listen not only determines what we hear, it also determines what people choose to tell us.

You're already listening. Right now. To something. There's no moment of being alive where you're not tuned to some frequency.

The question isn't how to start listening. The question is: what are you listening to?

Dazzle them

A while ago, one of our sales team came to me: 'I need you to come into a meeting tomorrow. Major client. Massive spender on your show and across the station. They're talking about cutting back their spending and moving it to a rival station'.

He looked at me with that desperate sales-guy energy. 'I need you to go in there and dazzle them.'

Dazzle them. Make them impressed. Perform. Win them over with my dazzling charm.

I didn't go in there and dazzle them.

But I did bring that room alive.

Here's what happened.

I caught myself doing what we all do: I was thinking too much about what I wanted to say. And in my head, I'd turned these people into some kind of flat, one-dimensional thing. A group out to get us. Doesn't like us anymore.

So I stopped. And I thought, *I'm going to put myself in their shoes.*

Why would they want to leave? Well, maybe we didn't do something well. Maybe it didn't work the way they hoped. Maybe we didn't listen hard enough to what they actually needed. Maybe this could be an opportunity to listen and have an honest conversation and be a problem solver.

So that's what I walked in planning to do. Not dazzle.

Connect. Understand. Serve.

I walked in. Sat down. The client's team looked guarded. Prepared for a pitch. The dazzler.

And I said, 'I get it. This obviously hasn't gone how you wanted it to. And I'm sorry if there was something we didn't understand or didn't fulfil'.

I could see the sales guy look at me like, *What the fuck are you doing? I told you to dazzle them, not help them out the door.*

But I kept going.

'I bet your business has changed since 12 months ago when we signed this deal. What's changed? What do you need your marketing to do now? What are you hoping is going to work at the other station?'

Silence for a second. Then they started talking.

And as they told me about how hard their business was, how the market had shifted, how their needs were different now, I said, 'Well, if we'd known that 12 months ago, I wouldn't have designed it like that. So if I was going to do it again — knowing what you actually need now — I'd do this, this and this'.

And I started coming up with ideas. Real-time. Unscripted. My creativity in the moment, responding to what they'd actually told me — not what I'd prepared to pitch.

They loved some of the ideas. We riffed on them. Built on them together.

Then something amazing happened.

Not only did they not cut their spend back — they increased it. They took even more out of the rival radio station.

No dazzle. Just listening.

Curiosity, not advice

Here's what most of us do: someone starts talking and within 30 seconds we're thinking, *I can fix this! How do I help? What's the solution? I know what you should do/think/feel.*

We think that's helpful. It's not. I'm so guilty of this pattern as a dad and husband. It's making it about us. About our wisdom. Our value. Our need to be useful.

Real listening is different. Real listening is curiosity. Listening in wonder.

Not 'How do I fix this?' but 'Tell me more'.

Not 'Here's what you should do' but 'What's that like for you?'

Not 'I understand' but 'Help me understand'.

When you drop your agenda and just get curious, something shifts. The person relaxes. They go deeper. They find their own answers.

Listening with curiosity is more powerful than giving advice.

The version they give you

Think about it like this.

If you're listening to fix, they'll give you the fixable version of the story. The version with a clear problem and a neat solution. The version that makes helping easy.

If you're listening to judge, they'll give you the defended version. The version where they're the hero, or at least not the villain. The version that protects them from your verdict.

If you're listening with genuine curiosity, with no agenda except to understand?

They'll give you the truth.

The messy version. The real version. The version they might not even know until they hear themselves say it.

That's what happened in that meeting. I wasn't listening to defend our position or overcome objections. I was listening to understand. So they gave me the truth about their business. And from that truth, solutions emerged.

People calibrate what they share based on how they're being received. Your listening creates the space—or closes it down.

The three channels

Deep listening isn't just about the other person. It's listening on three channels simultaneously.

Channel 1: Listening to yourself

What am I feeling right now? What's my body telling me? What's my truth?

Before that sales meeting I was tense, defensive, preparing to sell myself to them and rubbish the opposition. That noticing—that inner listening—is what allowed me to shift. Oftentimes, awareness is the key to our transformation.

Your body is a powerful antenna. A tuning fork for what's real and true. Your mind can lie to you. Your mind can rationalise. But your body always knows.

That tightness when something's off. That expansion when something's right. That sinking feeling when you're betraying yourself. That lift when you're in alignment.

Channel 2: Listening to them

What are they really saying beneath the words? What emotion do I sense? What do they need?

Not performing empathy. Actually tracking their experience.

In that meeting, when the clients started talking about how hard their business had become—how the market had shifted—I wasn't just hearing words. I was sensing their frustration, their fear, their hope that someone might actually understand.

That's what allowed genuine solutions to emerge. I wasn't responding to what they said. I was responding to what they meant.

Channel 3: Listening to what's emerging

What's the quality between us right now? Where does this conversation want to go? What's trying to emerge?

This is the channel most people miss entirely. But it's where the magic lives.

You understand a river by sitting beside it. Not by analysing it. You start noticing things—the eddies on the side, the flow in the middle, the different pace underneath versus on top. Stuff you can't grasp any other way.

Same with conversations. There's a river flowing. A direction the exchange wants to go. When you sense it and move with it, everything gets easier. When you fight it, you create friction.

In the sales meeting, I could feel the moment the energy shifted. When they stopped being defensive and started being honest. When the conversation stopped being about conflict and started being about collaboration. I didn't plan that. I felt it. And I moved with it.

Here's the trap. The more you try to *do* listening—to perform empathy, to fix, to prove your value—the more static you create.

Listening is pure receiving.

Receptive. Open. Effortless.

Thread-pulling questions

When you're really listening—on all three channels—questions arise naturally.

Not interrogation questions. Not 'let me show you how smart I am' questions. Not questions designed to steer them where you want them to go.

Thread-pulling questions.

The best questions come from genuine not-knowing. Questions you don't already have the answers to. Questions that pull a thread and see what unravels.

Here's something I learned from executive coach Joe Hudson: the difference between How/What questions and Why questions.

Why questions sound like accusations. 'Why did you do that?' carries judgement. It puts people on the back foot. They defend instead of discover.

How and What questions open things up. 'What led to that?', 'How did that feel?', 'What matters most here?' They invite exploration instead of defence.

In that sales meeting, I wasn't asking questions to overcome objections. I was pulling threads. 'What's changed in your business?', 'What do you need your marketing to do now?' Each answer revealed more. Each revelation opened the next question. Until we arrived somewhere none of us had planned to go — but all of us needed.

Great questions are like finding a loose thread and pulling gently. You watch what unravels. What reveals itself. What unfolds.

That's why I call the reflection prompts at the end of each chapter 'Unfolders'. Because the right question, asked with genuine curiosity, unfolds something that was folded. Opens what was closed. Reveals what was hidden.

When you're not listening

Here's a practice I've developed over the years: I try to notice when I'm not listening and understand why.

Because here's the thing: when your attention drifts, it's not random. It's information.

Someone's sharing something painful and suddenly I'm thinking about my shopping list. Why? Not because I'm a monster—because their pain just poked something in me I don't want to feel.

Someone's angry and I start planning my response. Why? Because their anger scares me and I want to defend.

Someone's being vulnerable and I go straight to problem-solving mode. Why? Because their vulnerability makes me feel helpless and I need to *do* something. Fix something. Anything, but just be there.

The moment you notice you're not listening, pause. Feel the emotion that's making you drift.

Not to judge it. Just to feel it.

And then, come back. Be here. Listen.

Feeling the emotion helps you return to true listening.

Listening as leadership

One realisation I've come to know is that I'm a better leader the more I listen. The more I speak last.

Not first. Last.

When I speak first, I set the agenda. I close down possibilities. Everyone else just responds to what I said.

When I speak last, I create space. I hear what's actually happening. I understand the field before I contribute to it.

The best teams are ones where people feel and know their voice matters. Where they are heard. Not just tolerated. Not just allowed to speak. Actually heard.

And that only happens when the leader listens first.

Google's Project Aristotle found that high-performing teams were ones where everybody felt comfortable speaking and contrary opinions were welcome. That only happens when people feel listened to.

Senior leaders who have peace in them are almost always exceptional listeners. They speak last in meetings. They know their opinion will influence others, so they create space for every voice first. Because intelligence is everywhere—if you learn to mine it by listening.

Listening while speaking

Here's the paradox: great speaking doesn't start with your mouth. It starts with your listening.

Half of my job—the creative work—is listening. Listening to what wants to come through. Listening to the callers. Listening to my team. Listening to the energy in the room.

You might think you stop listening when you speak. But you're always listening—the question is whether you're in that state of whole-body, present listening while you're talking.

When I'm in that deep form of listening and I'm talking at the same time, I'm curious about what's going to come out of my mouth. It's like I'm experiencing it for the first time. It feels like an unfolding, which delights me.

That's the unscripted moment. Words discovering themselves as they leave your mouth.

Listen first. Then speak.

Silent

Silent and *listen* are spelled with the same letters.

That's not a coincidence.

Real listening requires a kind of inner silence. A quietening of the voice that wants to respond, fix, impress, defend. A willingness to just… receive.

Listen to your life. It's speaking to you right now.

Listen to yourself. Your body, your intuition, your truth.

Listen to others. Not to fix. Not to advise. To receive them.

Listen with the ears of your heart.

Everything changes when you truly listen.

Unfolders

Three questions to sit with:

1. What are you listening to right now as you read this?
2. Who in your life needs you to just listen—not fix, not advise, just be with?
3. What might you hear if you stopped trying to listen...and just received?

14

You are a story

I love everything to do with stories and storytelling. My aim in this chapter is to give you a deeper understanding of the power of storytelling and share some ways you can find and tell better stories.

Every single day on my radio show, since the day I stumbled on air almost 30 years ago, I saw that everyday stories contain magic in the mundane. That's my catnip.

I also love the craft of it all. Deeply. My team would tell you that helping them get better at storytelling lights me up.

I wasn't always sure storytelling was my thing. In fact, I had no idea what my thing was.

My first ever radio boss was a crazy Australian called Steve. He took a huge chance on me—I had zero radio experience, and he put me on my first breakfast show. In those early days I was all over the place. Trying to be edgy. Doing poor topical jokes.

Then one day I told a story about an argument I'd had with my wife Sarah. A door-to-door salesman had arrived offering discounted pizza—weekly deliveries for the next three years. Sarah wasn't home. The deal seemed too good to refuse. I signed up on the spot.

When Sarah got back and found out I'd invested what little money we had in three years of weekly pizza, she was … erm … unimpressed. She called the company to get out of it. On the phone, she more or less suggested I was of low intelligence—a simpleton with learning difficulties—and shame on them for preying on such a simpering fool.

The next day, Steve called me into his office. Feet up on the desk, as always. He pointed a chewed pen at me and said, '*Maaaaattttte!* I almost crashed my car laughing at that pizza story. Who the fuck does that? Signs up for three farking years of pizza, ya boofhead?'

Then he said six words that changed everything: *You're a storyteller. That's your thing.*

At the time, I didn't fully understand what he meant. I was just sharing what happened to me. But Steve saw something I couldn't see yet.

'Come with me,' he said. I asked where we were going. He said he'd explain when we got there.

We walked to a cemetery.

Steve stopped among the headstones, put his hand on my shoulder and gestured at the hundreds of graves around us.

'All of these people,' he said, 'are dead'.

Steve had a habit of pointing out the blindingly obvious.

'And all of them died with their stories still in them.'

He looked at me.

'Your job isn't just to tell your stories. It's to give people permission to share theirs. That's what you do when you share yours.'

I've never forgotten that. Standing in a cemetery with a mad Australian, learning why stories matter.

Now, you might think, why does this matter to me.

It matters because everything is a story.

And stories are how we make sense of us, and the world.

This sacred primal technology is hardwired in all of us. Our original blueprint.

But you may have a script running about your ability to tell stories.

So, if you want to connect better at home, work or with friends, improving how you tell stories will have a big impact in all areas of your life. Coupled with understanding their power to transform us and the story listener — to inspire, take action, feel closer to the truth of who we are and what we are about.

First, let's kill a script together.

People say to me all the time, 'I don't have any stories'.

I used to nod sympathetically. Now I just smile and get excited about the discovery and memories they are about to have. Because 'I don't have any stories' is itself a story.

It's a story you've been telling yourself, probably for years. And it's not true. What you actually mean is, *I don't notice my stories.*

You have so many of them. They're happening to you every single day. You're just not paying attention. Or you've decided they don't count. That they're not dramatic enough, not interesting enough, not enough enough.

But here's what is true.

You are not a person who has stories. You are a story.

Stories are how we make sense of the world. They're how we've made sense of the world since we gathered around fires in caves. Before writing. Before schools. Before podcasts and TED Talks and keynote speeches. Before Insta reels and TikTok. There were people sitting in circles, sharing what happened to them. Did you know the oldest and most powerful form of storytelling is gossip? It's what kept tribes in line for so long without laws, the police or prisons.

Story is in our DNA.

Our minds aren't logic computers. They're story computers. We don't process life through data and spreadsheets and bullet points. We process it through narrative. Through characters and conflict and transformation.

You're doing it right now. You're making a story of this moment. Of reading this book. Of who you are and where you've been and where you might be going.

We are, all of us, story beings. Biologically hardwired for stories. It's not a skill to acquire. It's a primal inheritance and right to remember.

The Woodshed

One simple thing changed everything for me.

I created a place to collect my stories. Quickly. Easily. No pressure. No rules. No expectations. Just somewhere to dump the raw materials before I forget them.

I use the Notes app on my iPhone. If you're on Android, you'll have something similar. Create one note. Give it a name. Keep adding to it.

Mine is called The Woodshed.

It's where I store the stories. But here's the thing—I don't need them to be fully formed stories. They can be just a stack of kindling. A bit of wood. Raw materials I can build into a fire later.

I'm just gathering. I don't need to know what this is yet. That will come.

Here's an example.

I've just come back from a swim in the ocean with my wife. On the drive home, we got stuck behind an elderly couple driving on the main road in a golf cart.

I've never seen anything like it.

I'm not even sure it's legal. There's no way it's legal. No number plate, no rego. But it just seemed like this was a thing they did. Obviously, they were going really slowly, and they didn't care. There was something impressive about it, actually.

I have no idea what I'm going to do with that.

I don't need to know yet. Into The Woodshed it goes.

I'm looking at the note right now. Here's what I wrote:

Old couple. Golf cart. Main road. Didn't give a f.

Later, I'll start playing with it. Maybe there's something there about freedom. About what happens when you stop caring what people think. Maybe we should all just drive around our suburbs in golf carts. Be safer, wouldn't it? Friendlier. Less road rage, more conversation.

Or maybe it goes nowhere. Maybe it just stays kindling. Doesn't matter. Collect first, decide later.

The Woodshed takes the pressure off. You're not writing stories. You're noticing moments. You're paying attention to your life. And that alone changes something.

Stories in your back pocket

A lot of people have social anxiety. That low hum of dread before a dinner party, a work event, a gathering where you'll have to talk to people. And part of that anxiety is the fear that you'll have nothing to say. That you'll stand there with your drink, mind blank, while everyone else seems effortlessly interesting.

Here's something that could help.

Before you go out, have a look at your woodshed. Scan through it. Let a few stories land in you. Not to memorise. Not to rehearse. Just to have them available. Put a couple in your back pocket.

Then, when you're out with friends or strangers, you can weave them into conversation naturally. 'Oh, that reminds me of something that happened the other day…'

'What do you think of this that happened to me…?'

And suddenly you're not performing. You're sharing. You're connecting. I see them like sprinkling conversational acorns that might grow between you. Anything is better than the dreary, 'What do you do for a living?'

Golden stumbles

Often, we tend to bias stories where we have the upper hand. The polished ones. The semi-fabricated ones where we said that funny one-liner to the shopkeeper and everyone laughed. I'm not interested in those stories.

Tell me the story of when you fell over. When you slipped on life's banana skin.

I was staying in an Airbnb recently. The listing said it had a smart TV. I get into this place, sit down with a glass of wine, ready to watch something. I can't find the TV. I look everywhere. Nothing.

I contacted the superhost. 'There's no TV.'

She replies, very politely, 'The TV is on the wall'.

On the wall was a TV that I thought was a picture. It was one of those smart TVs that look like art when they're off.

Smart TV. Not-so-smart human.

That's the stuff. That's the gold. Not the story of how clever I was. The story of how I couldn't find a television that was right in front of my dumb face.

Your gold is in your stumbles. And your struggles.
The magic is in the mess.

When you think of a story and you think, 'I can't share that—it's too awkward, too messy, too embarrassing'. Know that signal, that ick, that inner cringe? That's exactly where you should go.

Remember: authenticity is vulnerability. It's courage. The courage to be you. The courage to tell your stories. The real ones. That's what we need. People's bullshit detectors are sharper than they've ever been. Start from truth.

I've got a story to share with you now.

My wife can't stand you

One night I was waiting in the green room to go on stage for my stand-up show. I was on tour. And I always love hearing the audience come in. Sometimes I go and hide behind the stage curtain just to listen.

There's this hubbub—that's the only word for it. This electricity that crackles through the room. They're excited. There's anticipation. The potential of the night. I love it. It lights me up. When I don't hear it, or it's muted, I get more concerned.

Anyway, I'm waiting in the green room. And stupidly, I go on my phone. I go on social media. Someone's sent me a DM.

Hey Christian, I'm coming to see you tonight. I'm a big fan. Nice, right?

Next line: *'Not my wife Diane, who is with me, she can't stand you'.*

I went from feeling like a king to an idiot in less than a second. Hero to zero. It was a gut punch. I felt my cheeks sting with shame.

She can't stand me. Why'd she even come? Don't come, Diane!

But then, straight away, this little thought popped up: that's the start of tonight's show. Find Diane.

My ego went, Oh, *don't do that. You can't say that. It hurts. It's embarrassing. Don't show the audience your weaknesses.*

But I did.

I started the show reading the message out loud.

Half the audience laughed. The other half went 'Ohhh' like my mum would—like it was mean, like they felt sorry for me.

I asked the guy where he was sitting. Found him. Found Diane. The poor woman had her head in her hands.

I said, 'Anyone else here like Diane tonight?'

Because I know what it's like when you go for a night out. There's the dragger and the dragee. The dragger is the person who wants to go, who bought the tickets, who's excited. And sometimes they're dragging another person along. A partner. A friend.

'Hands up, if you bought the ticket, you actually wanted to come see me.' People put their hands up.

'And hands up if you've been dragged along tonight.'

A whole other section raised their hands. And the room cracked open.

Suddenly there was this immediate, deeper connection. That show was such a wild ride. Because of the Dianes.

Opening with that vulnerability let me play with something real. I redirected the energy so it didn't shame me—I turned it into something else entirely. Something we were all in together.

I kept checking in with Diane throughout the show. 'Diane, how's it going?'

'Diane, out of 10, where are we at?'

Whenever a bit landed well, I'd say to someone in the front row, 'I don't have the guts to look at Diane—can you tell me, is she enjoying it?'

And then, as with any hour-long stand-up show, some bits stumbled. You breathe in on a punchline, and they don't quite hear the word. You improvise something in the moment, and it doesn't quite work. I love those bits, actually, because they create this awkward silence—and awkward silence is a chance to play.

There was one thing I said that got absolutely nothing. Just silence.

I walked off to get a drink of water from the stool on stage. And I just whispered into the microphone, 'What if Diane was right?'

Biggest reaction of the night.

What makes a story land

When I talk about landing, I'm talking about it landing me back into my heart. Real stories are felt.

They are not told from the head. Lead with logic and you'll be met with logic. Lead with your heart and you'll go straight into the hearts of others.

When I think about the stories that stay with me — the ones I remember, the ones that quietly changed and rearranged me — I notice they have three ingredients:

- *They are original.* Not original like 'never been done before'. Original like yours. Lived in your bones. Not borrowed from someone else's highlight reel. Your unique stories only you can tell.
- *There's some kind of struggle.* Something that wasn't easy. A hardship. A friction, a tension, a difficulty that had to be moved through.
- *There's a transformation.* Something shifted. Change happened. You came out different than you went in. Struggling creates transformation and that's how we learn.

I've interviewed Ricky Gervais many times over the years. Ricky is a world-class storyteller. Look at *The Office, Extras*. Look at *After Life*. My god, what a great story that is.

One time I was interviewing Ricky, and he said something so interesting. He said the best stories live in 'a very specific place'.

There's who we're trying to be — that version of ourselves we present to the world. And then there's who we really are.

The gap between those two? That's where all the great stuff is. I love that.

Now, here's what most people get wrong: they think the struggle has to be huge. A car crash. A divorce. A death. Some life-altering earthquake.

It doesn't. The struggle can be small. A moment with your kid that cracked you open. A conversation that didn't go the way you hoped. A stranger who said something that lodged in your chest. Getting stuck behind two old people in a golf cart and suddenly questioning your entire relationship with time and freedom.

Struggle doesn't have to be dramatic. It just has to be real.

And the transformation? That can be subtle too. Unfinished, even. Those are the stories I love most. The ones where you're still figuring it out. Where you used to think one thing and now, you're not so sure. Where you're passing on not a lesson but a question.

A good story can carry a lesson without ever announcing itself. It doesn't hit you over the head. It doesn't say 'This is the point'. If the story is honest enough, pure enough, the meaning finds its own way in.

Your story then meets my story and there is a kind of merging. Your story gets absorbed by the other person.

Witnessing, not preaching

Here's what I've learned about why the real stories land.

You're not preaching. You're witnessing.

You're saying, 'This is what I saw. This is what I felt. This is what I learned and I'm passing it on'.

And when you do that, something shifts in the listener. They stop hearing your story as your story. They start recognising themselves in it. They think, *Hang on... I've felt that too.*

That's the 'me too' moment. And it's extraordinary how often it happens—not because your life is unusual, but because you named something true.

They don't just hear your story—they realise they're not alone. You're giving words to what it is to be us. That's what I love about my job. That is my job.

Most people have no idea how powerful their own life experiences actually are. They've lived them … but they haven't worked with them. They haven't gone back and excavated their own story. Pulled it apart. Picked at it. Examined it.

They haven't stopped long enough to ask, 'What did this teach me? What did this show me about being human? What truth is hiding in here?'

When you do, and I hope you do, your life experiences can show you something about yourself and your true nature. They also do that for the listener. You can re-examine a moment in your life and look around, change the lens, widen the aperture and see something else. This reframing can give you a source of self-compassion and be the fuel for transformation.

Because the more attention you give to your own inner experience, the more energy you give to understanding and expressing what's happening inside you; and the more language you give it … the greater the gift you offer others.

The craft secret: Specificity

I took the great and wise Rob Bell to my favourite oak trees in Melbourne when he came on tour here. Under those trees magic happens. Rob felt it and said I should do a chat show under them! Anyway, we were swapping notes on storytelling, and we got to talking about what he calls the 'particulars' of your stories. The details matter. I call it 4k storytelling. We agreed that vagueness is the enemy of storytelling. The specifics and particulars are your best friend.

Not 'I was staying somewhere'—I was staying in an Airbnb. Not 'I couldn't find something'—I couldn't find the TV. Not 'I contacted someone'—I contacted the superhost. The details are what make it real. The details are what let people see it more vividly.

The more specific you are, the more universal it becomes.

Know your frequency

Every story carries a frequency. *Before I tell a story, I will take the time to really tune into its EFq, its emotional frequency. Then I'll tell the story from that frequency.*

Before you speak it, you need to know what it's tuned to.

Is this a story about grief? Joy? Loss? Resilience? Friendship? Belonging? Finding meaning? Becoming yourself again?

When you know the emotional frequency of your story, you stop performing. You start transmitting. And people don't just hear you—they *feel* you. Your story has much greater potency and power.

The story and what it's doing

Every story operates on two levels at once.

There's the surface. What happened. The events. The characters. The sequence of things.

And then there's what's running underneath. The depths. What the story is really about.

They run at the same time, but two layers. And when I tell a story I'm mining for the hidden gold that's deeper down. When I hear a story, I'm doing the same thing.

The surface of a story might be 'I moved house'. 'I gave away our family couch.'

But underneath? That's where the heart lives. That's where the magic is. Grief. Life. How we store our lives in objects. What happens when we have to let go.

Once you feel what's underneath your story, everything else becomes clear. You know what details matter. You know where to slow down. You know what to leave out. You're not just recounting events anymore—you're sharing something that resonates in a deeper place.

The best stories don't announce what they're about. They let you feel it.

Let me show you what I mean...

The couch of 1000 stories

We recently moved out of our family home. We'd been there seven years—ever since we came to Australia. And when you have a family, you know how much life happens in seven years. My daughters became teenagers in that house. They grew up. They left for university. The place had been a safe home for us. But now that they're gone, it feels more like a museum of what was than a house of what is. So, we're downsizing.

My wife Sarah and I went to do the final check. The place was empty. And my wife started to get emotional. It's time for us to close the door for the last time.

She goes, 'Chris, can you close the door? I just can't do it. I'm going to wait in the car. It's too much'.

And I see my wife walking down the path for the last time. She's sobbing.

I look through the hallway. The cat and the dog were always there. Noise. People. Energy. And now it's echoing. It's echoing.

As I'm closing the door, I feel like I'm really closing off a part of my life I can never go back to. Uncrossing a threshold I can't cross again.

But it doesn't make me sad. Not yet.

The next day, I don't know whether it's muscle memory, but I find myself not heading to my new home—I'm heading to my old one. Now, I could just turn off and correct this accident. But was it an accident? Something compels me. An impulse. To drive by the house.

Is it some part of me that wants to see the new people? Or is it some part of me that wants to really feel what I'm really feeling? To knock a scab off?

And sure enough, as I drive by so slowly—I'm almost at a standstill (okay, I was for a few seconds)—I see a dad walking into my house carrying a box.

I look down the hallway. And then I feel the tears.

Why did that make me sadder?

Here's what I think. When I closed that door, it was still my ending. The house was empty, but it was my empty. The echoes were my echoes. I was still the main character of that space.

But when I saw that dad carrying a box through my doorway, I realised the house had already moved on. It wasn't waiting for me. It wasn't grieving. It was already beginning someone else's story.

And I wasn't in it.

What hit me so viscerally was all this had happened so quickly—the last seven years and the new family moving in had all collapsed in time and space. How we don't have time; we are an expression of it.

There's one more part to this story.

We had a couch. We'd had that couch for over 10 years. From the UK to Australia. Birthdays. Christmases. Countless hours of watching TV. Laughing. Crying. Arguing. Making up. Sleeping. Napping. So much life happens on a couch when you think about it.

Have you ever thought about the significance of things? They hum with meaning.

When my first daughter moved out, a couple of days after she'd gone, I was sitting in my usual spot. We always have our usual spots on the family couch. Mine's grooved to my backside like a memory foam pillow.

And I found, shoved down the side of her cushion, a Calippo ice cream wrapper. I must have told her a million times, 'Put them in the bin'.

But seeing it there—shoved down the side—it brought tears to my eyes. It's a Calippo wrapper. But there's so much in it.

I'm just about to get up and put it in the bin. But I don't.

I shove it back down the side of the couch. I pat it. I hold it. It contains power. A connection to a time and place. To Ruby.

I put it back down there. So I can reach for it and find her again for a moment, back next to me on the couch.

The couch of 1000 stories was too big for the downsizing place, so I gave it away on my radio show for free. I just wanted a young family to have it and make their stories on it. I found one with two young daughters. Perfect.

Before they came to take the couch away, I retrieved that Calippo wrapper. I looked at it. I gave it a kiss.

And then I threw it away. I put it in the bin. I let it go. And a piece of my heart fell into the bin too.

Transformational stories

The kind of speaking I love most is transformational speaking. And really that means transformational storytelling.

This is when you don't just inform people—you shift them. Shapeshift them, in real time. It's like you're planting seeds. Seeds of possibility. Of hope. Of action. Of contemplation. This isn't about manipulating for personal gain.

Transformational speaking can only come from transformational stories. Stories that don't just entertain but change something in the person receiving them.

Remember the Peter Logan story in chapter 2?

A great example of transformational storytelling. That's how there was a 600 per cent increase in returned bowel cancer screening kits. Pete's authentic transformational story.

When we speak from the heart, authentically, it moves people. Not just to feel something—to do something. To change.

That's transformational storytelling. Not a polished presentation. Not a script. A man with terminal cancer, sitting in a radio studio, speaking from his chest instead of his notes, turning his mistake into meaning.

Keep up the humour, don't forget the human.

Some stories stay with you a lifetime. Pete's will.

I'd love to help you find your transformational stories.

They will come from deep within you. And you'll know when you find them. They embody what you care about most. They carry the weight of what actually matters to you.

You are the expert in your life. No-one else has lived it. As AI gets better at churning out stories, your edge is your authentic realness. This is how to fast-track connection and rapport. No-one else knows what you know. Has known your struggles, how you overcame them. Which means no-one else can tell the stories that are yours to tell.

So, I invite you to excavate your life experience. Be an adventurer. An explorer of your own inner world and biography.

Think of times when life surprised you. What did you do to overcome this? Your struggles and hardships are rich stories in waiting. They help you make meaning of your life and how you tell the story you get to control. What was once an awful time can now become a story that's about your courage and determination, and what you learned about yourself. How that influences how you show up now.

Dare, like Indiana Jones, to go to those places you've hidden away. The parts you left behind. The parts you exiled. The parts you—like me—boarded over in order to fit in.

That's where the magic is. In your mess.

The three Hs

When I first came to Australia, I inherited a team who didn't know me and weren't particularly invested in the show's success. Or in me. There was a distance between us. Arms folded. Walls up.

And of course, the fastest way to form connection is vulnerability. To me, the currency of storytelling is vulnerability.

So, I tried something. I invited each person to tell a story about three things: a hero in their life, a hardship they'd faced and a highlight they were proud of.

Hero. Hardship. Highlight.

Simple framework. Profound results.

There wasn't a single person—including me—who didn't shed a tear sharing their stories. We started with arms folded and disconnected. We ended with hugging and a depth of connection I couldn't have created any other way.

That's what happens when you share real stories. The walls come down. The masks slip off. And suddenly you're not colleagues or acquaintances or strangers anymore. You're humans who have seen each other. You allowed the real self to speak up and out, and in that act, the new story of you emerges calling you on. Whispering: 'scrap the script'.

To help you mine your life, you can download a Story Mining PDF Guide and some Triple H stories from www.christianoconnell.com/unscript

Why we really tell stories

When I was writing my first two children's books, I had this great editor, Nick. A hugely talented writer himself. He told me something that's never left me.

He said that when publishers really examine bestselling books—look at what they have in common across genres, across age groups—the most important theme isn't adventure. It isn't magic. It isn't even triumph.

It's human closeness. Connection.

The stories we return to again and again—the ones that get passed down and read out loud and held onto—they make us feel less alone. They remind us of our sacred togetherness.

That makes perfect sense, doesn't it?

Great storytelling is really an investigation into us. What it is to be human. How we behave. How we love and fail and try again. How we hurt each other and find our way back.

The gift of a story is wisdom being passed on. Not wisdom like 'Here's the answer'. Wisdom like 'Here's what happened to me, and maybe it means something to you too'.

When we tell a story authentically—and I've seen this happen even when the story you're handling is very particular and personal—the listener finds themselves in your story even if their situation is totally different.

Heart to heart

I love storytelling because it bypasses the noise in your head and goes straight to your heart. That's where authentic connection lives. So much communication now on podcasts and social media is people trying to impress someone with how very clever and smart they are, brain to brain.

Stories bypass the monkey mind.

There's a quote by the psychologist James Hillman that I like:

> *We are not the experience of our lives. We are the stories we tell about them.*

Your life doesn't mean anything until you make meaning of it. And you make meaning through story. Through the telling. Through the shaping. Through deciding what it was about.

You can change the script you have about you and your life at any time and become the new story of you.

A great story shouldn't tell you what to think. It's like a canvas that you colour in yourself. Because every time I tell a story, three different people will have three different reactions. We bring ourselves to every story we receive. We find what we need to find.

The new story of you

Here's a question I want to leave you with: What's your new story of you?

Not the old story. The one you've over-told. Over and over to yourself. The one that's easy to hide behind. The comfortable narrative you've been recycling for years.

What's the story that's emerging right now? The one you're still in the middle of? The one that scares you a little because you don't know how it ends? I'm guessing it might be about the threshold/s in some area of your life you are in right now.

That's the story worth telling. That's the story worth finding. That's what the world needs.

Share your good gift, the gift of your real stories.

Steve was right. People die with their stories still in them.

Yours don't have to be one of them.

Unfolders

Questions to sit with:

1. What do you think the story about the couch is also doing?
2. Think of a story you've told many times. Now ask, What's that story really about? What's underneath the events?
3. What are your three Hs? Who was a hero in your life, what is a hardship you've faced and what is a highlight you're proud of?

Conclusion

Talking each other home

I need to tell you about the week that changed everything.

After seven years of broadcasting to Melbourne, I was about to go national. In January 2026, our show would launch across every major Australian city. But before that happened, I had a plan.

Australian radio shuts down for the holidays. The last shows of 2025 aired on Friday, 12 December. Every rival breakfast show went on vacation. The airwaves went quiet.

Which meant there was an opportunity.

I'd fly to Sydney and broadcast a secret week of shows—just for them. While everyone else was on holiday, I'd introduce myself to a city that didn't know me yet. Say hello.

That was the idea. What happened was something else.

* * *

We flew in on Sunday, 14 December.

That evening, the team gathered for dinner. Drinks, laughter, excitement. We talked through the week ahead—the segments we'd prepared, the surprises we had planned.

And then, one by one, our phones started pinging.

At first, just fragments. Something happening at Bondi Junction. Reports unclear. Then more details. Multiple casualties. Then the number kept climbing.

Six people dead. Families out shopping. Lives ended in minutes.

The restaurant went quiet. Other tables checking their phones. The same disbelief rippling outward, table by table, face by face.

I looked up and saw my team looking at me. They weren't just frightened about what had happened. They were frightened about what we were supposed to do next.

Someone asked the question no-one wanted to say out loud: 'Should we even do this?'

I reassured them. 'We've got this.'

They didn't believe it.

'I've got this.'

I'm not sure I did.

* * *

I didn't sleep that night.

I lay in the dark, running through every possible version of the next morning, and none of them worked. The scripts I'd prepared now seemed obscene—bright, polished introductions for a city that was devastated.

At one point I caught myself spiralling—*Who am I to do this?*—and then I stopped.

I shifted the lens. From me. To them. To being of service.

When I get nervous, I focus on service.

Lying there, I heard an ambulance racing by, and I thought of Rob.

* * *

If you read the opening of this book, you know about Rob—the paramedic who came when my mother-in-law Jackie collapsed.

Rob couldn't save her life. But instead of rushing out, he stayed. He helped us move Jackie into her bed, so Sarah could have those precious hours lying beside her mum. He treated us like humans, not a situation to be processed.

That night in Sydney, I realised that's what I needed to do too. Be present, and with an open heart. Get out of my head. Not perform. Just show up.

* * *

Six am came round quickly.

Before that, I arrived at a station I'd never been in. The building rose 17 floors. At the top was a studio overlooking Sydney's Harbour Bridge. Everything seemed so big—the building, the city, the challenge.

I threw up outside the Coca-Cola building next to a giant Santa. I'm very sorry.

The microphone went live.

And I threw away everything I'd prepared.

'I'm sorry we meet this way.'

Six words. They weren't clever. They weren't polished. They were just true.

I told them I'd hoped our first week together could be something different. That I'd imagined introducing myself properly. Earning their trust slowly.

And then I said what I actually felt: that I hoped, in the days ahead, our show could be a place of hope. Support. Comfort.

I had planned an introduction. What I got was an initiation.

* * *

What happened that week still moves me.

I've been in radio since 1998. That week in Sydney will go down as the single most heartbreaking, intense and profoundly rewarding of my career.

The calls came. Not the usual calls—these were different. People needed to talk. To process. To hear another voice and know they weren't alone.

One listener wrote: 'You came on at possibly the worst time in recent history. I was going to look for a new show but I was wrong. This week, you have shown empathy, sympathy and humour in the right places'.

Another said we had 'gently ushered them through the week, giving us space to cry and grieve, time to smile and see hope and light—and even opportunities to laugh through the darkness'.

They weren't responding to my preparation. They were responding to my presence.

So much of the speaking we hear—and do ourselves—is synthetic. Right now, we don't need polyester people.

That week showed me how much we need each other. How starved we are for real contact. How desperate we are to feel less alone.

* * *

A listener named Brad wrote to tell me about the blood bank at Parramatta. The queue stretched outside. It took him and his wife an hour and a half just to reach the reception desk.

'Christian, in that queue almost every nationality and occupation was represented. Arabic, Indian, Korean, Aussie tradies, young girls in activewear, executives—folks from every walk of life, all there together.'

A short, elderly couple stood waiting patiently. The husband wore his yarmulke. They'd been turned away at Bondi—the lines were too long—so they'd driven across the city to try again.

The man in front of Brad had taken time off work to donate. He was wearing an Indigenous printed jumper over his uniform — clearly a police officer. Brad asked how he was travelling.

The officer answered quietly, 'The Rabbi that died was our chaplain'.

After waiting all that time, Brad was told he'd have to come back tomorrow at 7 am.

'No problem,' he said. 'See you then.'

Brad's last line says it better than I could: 'Everyone patiently waited to be part of the solution and not part of the problem'.

We are hardwired to come together. Unity is the felt experience of not being separate.

And to top it all off, someone made me a cake and brought it to the station at 6 am. Baking is caring — title of my next book.

* * *

There's a word I learned years ago from a conversation with a vet in a country pub: *philopatry.*

It's the instinct animals have that guides them home after long migrations. Salmon swimming upstream. Birds crossing continents. Something encoded deep in their cells that whispers: *This way, keep going, you're almost home.*

We're all trying to find our way home. That ache is in every story we love, every song that makes us cry without knowing why. The search for home. The longing to feel at one with ourselves, and with each other.

But here's what I've learned: you cannot come home alone.

We need each other — not as teachers or saviours, but as reminders. Fellow travellers who say, 'I see you. Keep going. I'm right here'.

The spiritual teacher Ram Dass said we are all just walking each other home.

I think what's also true is *We are just talking each other home.*

Eulogy lessons

After Jackie died, my wife asked me to deliver her eulogy.

She was 75 when she moved to Australia, leaving behind everything she knew. And in those final years, she built a whole new life. New friends, new community, new purpose.

The church was packed. All those people — and she'd met every one of them after 75.

Jackie had given herself a job at the church. A volunteer position. She became what she called a greeter.

A greeter stands outside before the service begins. They watch the people walking by — strangers, mostly — and offer a kind invitation. Not pushy. Just warm. *You're welcome here. Come in if you'd like.*

A greeter makes no assumptions. They don't wait for people to prove themselves worthy of welcome. They simply stand at the door and say, *I see you. There's a place for you here.*

I think about greetings a lot now. The ones we offer others. And the ones we offer ourselves.

* * *

In Ireland, in a dark, fire-lit pub, I was talking to David Whyte about my work. He listened intently, then said in that deep voice, 'Marvellous, marvellous. The mark of any authentic work in the world is ... generosity'.

We talked about what makes a great conversation. That word kept showing up. Generosity. And its companion: invitation.

Generosity is giving more than you normally might. Staying a little longer. Listening a little deeper. Offering something of yourself without knowing if you'll get anything back.

Invitation is how generosity travels. It doesn't push. It opens. It says, *Here's a door, come through if you'd like.*

The best conversations have both. That's what this book has tried to be. Not instructions. Not answers. Just a generous invitation to come home to yourself.

Before you go...

I've just been out for a walk. Among trees, of course.

This year, our younger daughter was the last to leave home. It's a privilege to watch your children go out into the world. But it's also hard. There's nothing that demands more vulnerability than becoming a parent.

With us being back to just the two of us—Sarah and me—it felt like pieces of our hearts walked out that door.

This was a tremendously bleak way to see it. And it is, of course, a story. A script.

But in sitting down to write this book, I realised something. It allowed me to kill an old script. The empty nest script. And in its place begins a new story.

I also realised that everything I've been saying to you, I've been saying to me. At exactly the right time. Our conversations really helped put me back into my heart.

Back home, in me.

Throughout writing this book, every word has been spoken out loud first. I've never written a book like that. Every word on these pages came out of my mouth before it hit the page.

I share this because I really have had a sense that I'm talking to you. And I hope, when you've been reading, it's felt like we're in a conversation together.

I've enjoyed walking side by side. Talking each other home.

Big love,

Christian

If something landed or shifted or surprised you, tell me. You're part of this conversation. christian@christianoconnell.com

Acknowledgements

This book wouldn't exist without Jordon Lott. She believed in *Unscript* when it was still just an idea and a dream. This is a very different kind of book for me to write, and her joyous energy and sharp insight helped shape it into what it is. To Jordon and her team at Wiley publishing—thank you for taking the leap with me.

Thank you to Ruby O'Connell for her honest/brutal feedback and notes, which at times were like very painful deep-tissue massages for my ego. Lois O'Connell for giving me hope this might be a decent book after reading a chapter and complimenting its 'shocking level of wisdom'. Like it didn't make sense from the dad she's known. My wife Sarah for giving me the space to write this in a very busy time in our lives.

To the trees and land of Red Hill on the Mornington Peninsula—the traditional Country of the Bunurong/Boon Wurrung people of the Kulin Nation: I wrote much of this book beneath those trees, on land that has been cared for over 40 000 years. I pay my respects to Elders past, present and emerging, and thank them for the stillness and wisdom their land offered me.

Thanks to the poet and philosopher David Whyte, whose work has inspired me deeply as a person and broadcaster.

To my mentors here in Australia, who helped me find my footing on new ground: Sara Brooke, Dean Benson and the Dragons, and Monique Elouise. You saw me when I couldn't see myself.

To Joe Hudson, whose work challenged me, cracked me open and still does: fuck you, Joe!

To the effervescent and wise Ben Crowe, who inspired me to begin mentoring and coaching others—to pass the gift forward.

And to everyone who took the time to email me after reading *No One Listens to Your Dad's Radio Show*: you probably don't know this, but those messages helped walk me back home. They are part of the reason this book exists.

Thank you.

References

Chapter 1

Harvard Study of Adult Development (1938–present): The longest-running study of human happiness, tracking 724 people across their entire lives. Findings published in: Waldinger, R. J., & Schulz, M. S. (2023). *The Good Life: Lessons from the World's Longest Scientific Study of Happiness*. Simon & Schuster.

US Surgeon General Advisory on Loneliness: Murthy, V. H. (2023). *Our Epidemic of Loneliness and Isolation: The U.S. Surgeon General's Advisory on the Healing Effects of Social Connection and Community*. US Department of Health and Human Services. (81-page report stating health risks of loneliness equivalent to smoking 15 cigarettes a day.)

'The Anti-Social Century' article: Thompson, D. (2025). *The Atlantic*. (Statistics on increased alone time and restaurant takeout trends.)

Marc Dunkelman's 'Three Rings' concept: Dunkelman, M. (2014). *The Vanishing Neighbor: The Transformation of American Community*. W. W. Norton, & Company. (Research on inner, middle and outer rings of connection.)

7 per cent communication statistic (Albert Mehrabian): Mehrabian, A. (1971). *Silent Messages: Implicit Communication of Emotions and Attitudes*. Wadsworth. (Note: Often oversimplified; applies specifically to communication of feelings and attitudes.)

Neuroscience of voice and connection: Various studies on voice processing and oxytocin release, including Seltzer, L. J., Ziegler, T. E., & Pollak, S. D. (2010). Social vocalizations can release oxytocin in humans. *Proceedings of the Royal Society B, 277*(1694), 2661–2666.

Nicholas Epley's Train Experiments: Epley, N., & Schroeder, J. (2014). Mistakenly Seeking Solitude. *Journal of Experimental Psychology: General, 143*(5), 1980–1999. Also discussed in Epley, N. (2014). *Mindwise: How We Understand What Others Think, Believe, Feel, and Want.* Knopf.

Chapter 2

Billy Connolly: Scottish comedian known for his unscripted, improvisational performance style. Multiple documentaries and performances available.

Martin Luther King Jr's 'I Have a Dream' speech (28 August 1963): Lincoln Memorial, Washington D.C. Historical accounts of Mahalia Jackson's encouragement and the improvised nature of the famous refrain.

Clarence B. Jones. King's speechwriter and advisor, present at the 1963 speech: Jones, C. B., & Connelly, S. (2011). *Behind the Dream: The Making of the Speech that Transformed a Nation.* Palgrave Macmillan.

Chapter 4

Jerry Seinfeld quote: 'A few seconds of weightlessness.' From author's personal interview with Seinfeld, discussing the experience of making someone laugh. From his promo tour of *Bee Movie.* From *The Christian O'Connell Breakfast Show,* Absolute Radio.

Joe Hudson (executive coach): Referenced as source for the thought experiment on connection's value. Hudson is founder of the Art of Accomplishment program.

Harvard Study of Adult Development (referenced again): Additional findings on relationship quality predicting health outcomes at age 80.

Chapter 6

Princeton neuroscience research on storytelling and brainwave synchronisation: Stephens, G. J., Silbert, L. J., & Hasson, U. (2010). Speaker–listener neural coupling underlies successful communication. *Proceedings of the National Academy of Sciences, 107*(32), 14425–14430.

Jerry Seinfeld on stand-up as surfing: Various interviews where Seinfeld compares performing to surfing, including *Comedians in Cars Getting Coffee* and Howard Stern interviews.

Joe Hudson's VIEW framework: Hudson, J. (2023). Art of Accomplishment program. Framework includes Vulnerability, Impartiality, Empathy, Wonder.

Chapter 7

Dacher Keltner's research on awe: Keltner, D. (2023). *Awe: The New Science of Everyday Wonder and How It Can Transform Your Life.* Penguin Press. Research conducted at UC Berkeley finding awe as strongest predictor of health among positive emotions.

Rob Bell on spirituality: Referenced regarding Hebrew scriptures and the Moses/burning bush interpretation. Bell, R. Various writings and podcasts.

Chapter 8

David Whyte, poet and philosopher: Referenced in connection with author's walking tour in Ireland and the quote, 'Nature reminds us to leave ourselves alone, just to be unutterably ourselves.'

John O'Donohue quote: 'Music is what language aspires to be.' From interview on Krista Tippett's podcast *On Being.*

Keltner's Eight Wonders of Life: Moral beauty, collective effervescence, nature, music, visual design, spirituality and religion, life and death, and epiphany.

Chapter 10

Joe Hudson's Art of Accomplishment: Referenced for insights on enjoyment and presence in communication.

Chapter 11

Roger Federer interview: Referenced for quote about his greatest achievement being longevity and love of the game.

Chapter 12

Jerry Seinfeld joke on public speaking: Classic bit about public speaking being feared more than death, meaning people at funerals would rather be in the coffin than giving the eulogy.

UCLA research on affect labelling: Lieberman, M. D., et al. (2007). Putting Feelings into Words: Affect Labeling Disrupts Amygdala Activity in Response to Affective Stimuli. *Psychological Science, 18*(5), 421–428. (Research showing that naming emotions calms the amygdala.)

The story of Milarepa and the demons: Traditional Tibetan Buddhist teaching story about the 11th-century yogi Milarepa. Various retellings, including Trungpa, C. (1973). *Cutting Through Spiritual Materialism*. Shambhala.

Sarah Lewis on archery and mastery: Lewis, S. (2014). *The Rise: Creativity, the Gift of Failure, and the Search for Mastery*. Simon & Schuster. (Concepts of 'split vision' and 'gold fever' / 'target panic'.)

Professor Andrew Huberman's 'physiological sigh' technique (double breath): Huberman, A. Huberman Lab Podcast and Stanford research on breathing techniques for stress reduction.

Chapter 13

Joe Hudson on listening: Referenced for insights on the quality of listening determining what people share.

Google's Project Aristotle: Duhigg, C. (2016). What Google learned from its quest to build the perfect team. *The New York Times Magazine* (findings on psychological safety in high-performing teams).

Chapter 14

Ricky Gervais on storytelling: Author's personal interviews with Gervais. Quote about best stories living in 'a very specific place'. *The Christian O'Connell Breakfast Show*, Absolute Radio.

James Hillman quote: Hillman, J. (1996). *The Soul's Code: In Search of Character and Calling*. Random House (referenced regarding stories and identity).